THE ULTIMATE
CRYSTAL PALACE FC
TRIVIA BOOK

A Collection of Amazing Trivia Quizzes
and Fun Facts for Die-Hard Eagles Fans!

Ray Walker

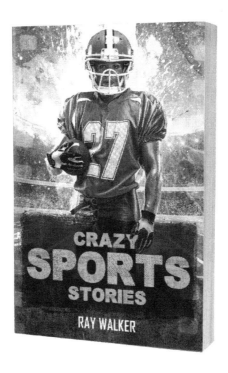

CONTENTS

INTRODUCTION

Although Crystal Palace FC was officially founded in 1905 as a hobby for the Crystal Palace Company's cricket players, the club's roots stretch back to 1861 when the amateur Crystal Palace team was in existence.

Either way, it's been well over a century now and fans have witnessed the side progress through the ranks of the Southern League and English Football League to reach the pinnacle known as the Premier League.

First nicknamed the "Glaziers", and later the "Eagles" by their passionate fans, the club has suffered ups and downs along the way but has seemingly found a deserving home in the top tier of English soccer.

The team is known for its determined effort on the pitch game after game and has thrilled its fans in FA Cup finals and several other domestic competitions.

Crystal Palace supporters have had the pleasure of witnessing some of the world's top players and managers in action for their club throughout the years with numerous colorful figures such as Ian Wright, Mark Bright, Wilfried Zaha, Andy Johnson, Johnny Byrne, Dougie Freedman, Peter Simpson, Ted Smith,

Clinton Morrison, Dwight Gayle, George Clarke, Albert Harry, Nigel Martyn, Jim Cannon, Julián Speroni, Kenny Sansom, Geoff Thomas, Peter Taylor, John "Jack" Robson, Steve Coppell, Tony Pulis, Dave Bassett, Attilio Lombardo, Ted Birnie, Gareth Southgate, Mile Jedinak, Tony Popovic, and Hayden Mullins.

This up-to-date trivia book has been written to celebrate the club's wonderful history from day one until the end of the 2020-21 Covid-19-affected campaign. You'll be able to meet and read about the team's top players and managers and how each of them left an everlasting effect on the club.

Crystal Palace's fascinating story is told here in educational quiz form, with 12 unique chapters each representing a different topic. All sections feature 20 stimulating quiz questions along with 10 intriguing "Did You Know" facts. The questions are presented in 15 multiple-choice and 5 true-or-false options, with the answers presented on a separate page.

This is the ideal way to test yourself on the ongoing flight of the Eagles and to challenge fellow Palace fans and other soccer supporters to quiz showdowns. The book will help refresh your knowledge of your favorite team and help you prepare for all challenges.

CHAPTER 1:

ORIGINS & HISTORY

QUIZ TIME!

1. Although the amateur Crystal Palace club was formed in 1861, Crystal Palace FC was officially founded in what year?

    a. 1900
    b. 1905
    c. 1875
    d. 1863

2. The club turned professional in 1905.

    a. True
    b. False

3. What was the club's original nickname before being changed to the Eagles?

    a. The Founders
    b. The Guards
    c. The Fairs
    d. The Glaziers

4. What was the first league the team played in professionally?

   a. The Football League
   b. The Combination
   c. The Southern League
   d. The Western League

5. Which club did Crystal Palace play in their first Southern League game?

   a. Sheffield FC
   b. Forest FC
   c. Southampton Reserves
   d. London FC

6. What has been Palace's stadium home since 1924-25?

   a. Croydon Common Athletic Ground
   b. Selhurst Park
   c. Hyde Park
   d. Crystal Palace Park

7. The amateur Crystal Palace club was a founding member of the Football Association in 1863.

   a. True
   b. False

8. What was the first season the club reached the top-tier First Division of the Football League?

   a. 1922-23
   b. 1953-54

c. 1969-70

d. 1977-78

9. What was the team's original kit color before turning professional?

a. Red

b. Amber and claret

c. Navy blue and black

d. Light blue and white

10. What design did the club feature on its shirts before a proper crest was introduced in 1944?

a. The name of a local tavern believed to be the first-ever kit sponsorship

b. The club's initials, "CPFC"

c. The Selhurst coat of arms

d. The player's name followed by their designated position

11. Which side did Palace play in their first match in the Football League?

a. Merthyr Town FC

b. Southend United

c. Bristol Rovers FC

d. Swansea City FC

12. Palace was a founding member of the Premier League.

a. True

b. False

13. What was the outcome of the squad's first Southern League match?

   a. 3-0 win

   b. 1-0 win

   c. 3-4 loss

   d. 2-2 draw

14. Which year did the club introduce its red and blue shirts?

   a. 1965

   b. 1973

   c. 1977

   d. 1980

15. Which team did the Eagles meet in their first Premier League game?

   a. Oldham Athletic

   b. Norwich City FC

   c. Tottenham Hotspur

   d. Blackburn Rovers

16. The original amateur Crystal Palace club was founded in 1861 by a group of cricketers playing for the Crystal Palace Company who wanted something to do during the winter.

   a. True

   b. False

17. What was the outcome of Crystal Palace's first Premier League match?

a. 1-1 draw

b. 0-4 loss

c. 3-3 draw

d. 1-2 loss

18. The Crystal Palace amateur club played in which historic tournament?

    a. The first friendly match against the original English men's national team
    b. The first FA Charity Shield game
    c. The first game played under floodlights
    d. The first-ever FA Cup in 1871-72

19. The team won its first Premier League game against which club?

    a. Wimbledon FC
    b. Everton FC
    c. Queens Park Rangers
    d. Arsenal FC

20. The Crystal Palace National Sports Centre was used to host FA Cup final matches from 1895 to 1914.

    a. True
    b. False

QUIZ ANSWERS

1. B – 1905

2. A – True

3. D – The Glaziers

4. C – The Southern League

5. C Southampton Reserves

6. B – Selhurst Park

7. A – True

8. C – 1969-70

9. D – Light blue and white

10. B – The club's initials, "CPFC."

11. A – Merthyr Town FC

12. A – True

13. C – 3-4 loss

14. B – 1973

15. D – Blackburn Rovers

16. A – True

17. C – 3-3 draw

18. D – The first-ever FA Cup tournament

19. B – Everton FC

20. A – True

DID YOU KNOW?

1. The Crystal Palace Football Club currently competes in the top-tier English Premier League and plays its home matches at Selhurst Park, in the borough of Croydon in South London, which has a capacity of just over 26,000 fans. The club was officially formed in 1905 and its nicknames are the Eagles and the Glaziers; however, many fans simply refer to the team as "Palace." The club's owners are listed as Steve Parish of England and Americans Joshua Harris and David S. Blitzer, with Parish serving as chairman.

2. Although the official founding date of the club is Sept. 10, 1905, under the guidance of Aston Villa assistant secretary Edmund Goodman, the club itself claims to be a continuation of the original amateur Crystal Palace Football Club, which was established in 1861. Both the amateur and professional teams played their home games at the Crystal Palace Exhibition venue and the professional side used the stadium for home contests until 1915.

3. The Crystal Palace Company originally formed a football club for its cricket players in 1861 and played its first game on March 15 against Forest FC. The amateur Crystal Palace club was an original founding member of the English Football Association in 1863 and competed in the first-ever FA Cup tournament in 1871-72. However, the

team disappeared from historical records following the 1875-76 FA Cup.

4. In 1895, the Crystal Palace Company built a soccer stadium named the Crystal Palace National Sports Centre, which hosted FA Cup finals from 1895 to 1914, and the club's amateur games resumed. From 1901-02 onward, the company's employees led a campaign to turn the team professional. The Crystal Palace Football Club then became professional under the ownership of a separate limited company, with the Crystal Palace Company as the majority shareholders.

5. The club applied for election into the Football League but was rejected and then joined the Second Division of the Southern League in 1905-06. They also played in the mid-week United Counties League. Their first professional match was on Sept. 2, 1905, when they were beaten 4-3 by Southampton Reserves at the Crystal Palace. The team didn't lose another match for the rest of the season and was crowned champions to earn promotion to the Southern League's First Division.

6. After World War I broke out in 1914, the club was forced to leave its Crystal Palace venue and play its home matches at Herne Hill, the home of West Norwood FC. In 1918, the team moved to a new stadium in Selhurst named The Nest. This was originally the home of the Croydon Common club, which had recently folded.

7. The club eventually joined the Third Division of the Football League in 1920-21 and won the division to earn promotion to the Second Division. Since then, the club has generally competed in the top two tiers of English soccer. Since 1963-1964, the Eagles have dropped below the second tier just once, for three seasons from 1974-75 through 1976-77.

8. Palace moved to a new soccer stadium named Selhurst Park in 1924 and their first match there was played on August 30, a 1-0 defeat to Sheffield Wednesday. The land for the new ground was purchased in 1922 for £2,570 and it cost £30,000 to erect the stadium.

9. The Eagles achieved their highest league finish ever in 1990-91 by placing third in the top-tier First Division. However, the team failed to qualify for the UEFA Cup at the end of the campaign due to the limited number of spots available to English clubs after the lifting of the UEFA ban, which was the result of the Heysel Stadium disaster in May 1985 in Brussels, Belgium.

10. Crystal Palace was a founding member of the Premier League, which began competition in 1992-93. The club was relegated in 1997-1998 and suffered financial difficulties that resulted in the club going into administration in 1999 and 2010. However, it recovered and returned to the Premier League in 2013-14 and has remained there ever since as of 2021-22.

CHAPTER 2:

ODDS & ENDS

QUIZ TIME!

1. How many games did Palace win in its first season in the Southern League?

    a. 10
    b. 16
    c. 19
    d. 22

2. The club's first legitimate crest was a claret and blue shield inside an outline of the Crystal Palace.

    a. True
    b. False

3. What was the first European competition the Eagles played in?

    a. UEFA Intertoto Cup
    b. UEFA-Cities Fairs Cup
    c. The European Cup
    d. Anglo-Italian Cup

4. Which was the first team Palace played at Selhurst Park?

   a. Wimbledon FC
   b. Sheffield Wednesday FC
   c. Leicester City FC
   d. Everton FC

5. Who was the youngest player to play for Crystal Palace, at the age of 15 years and 287 days?

   a. Wayne Routledge
   b. Alex Wynter
   c. Paul Hinshelwood
   d. John Bostock

6. How many games did the team win in its first season in the Football League?

   a. 9
   b. 14
   c. 18
   d. 24

7. For nearly a decade, Crystal Palace had a bald eagle as a mascot that would fly from end-to-end of Selhurst Park before home matches.

   a. True
   b. False

8. Who was the first Palace player to be capped by an international team?

   a. Wilf Innerd
   b. Jimmy Bauchop

c. Billy Davies

d. Horace Colclough

9. What season was Palace relegated?

a. 1920-21

b. 1924-25

c. 1933-34

d. 1956-57

10. Who was the club's winner of the Young Player of the Year award in 1983?

a. Dave Lindsay

b. Gary Stebbing

c. Billy Gilbert

d. Paul Hinshelwood

11. How many games did the Eagles draw in their first season in the top tier of the Football League?

a. 10

b. 4

c. 15

d. 0

12. Crystal Palace lost just one game in its first season in the Southern League.

a. True

b. False

13. Who was the oldest player to make an appearance for the team, at the age of 41 years and 68 days?

a. Kevin Phillips
b. Andy Linighan
c. Julián Speroni
d. Jack Little

14. What was the first club Palace played in a UEFA-sanctioned European tournament?

a. Samsunspor
b. FC Vorskla Poltava
c. FC Zbrojovka Brno
d. Austria Wien

15. How many games did the squad win in its first Premier League season?

a. 6
b. 8
c. 11
d. 15

16. Famous football stadium architect Archibald Leitch designed Selhurst Park.

a. True
b. False

17. The A23/M23 Derby is the name for the rivalry between Crystal Palace and which club?

a. Brighton & Hove Albion
b. Charlton Athletic
c. Millwall FC
d. AFC Wimbledon

18. How many times has the club been relegated?

    a. 8

    b. 6

    c. 5

    d. 3

19. Who was the first player to be used as a substitute for the club?

    a. Bert Howe

    b. Ronnie Allen

    c. Keith Smith

    d. Brian Wood

20. Palace has been relegated from the Premier League five times.

    a. True

    b. False

QUIZ ANSWERS

1. C – 19

2. A – True

3. D – Anglo-Italian Cup

4. B – Sheffield Wednesday FC

5. D – John Bostock

6. D – 24

7. A – True

8. C – Billy Davies

9. B – 1924-25

10. B – Gary Stebbing

11. C – 15

12. A – True

13. D – Jack Little

14. A – Samsunspor

15. C – 11

16. A – True

17. A – Brighton and Hove Albion

18. A – 8

19. C – Keith Smith

20. B – False

DID YOU KNOW?

1. The Herne Hill Velodrome in Herne Hill, South London, built in 1891, is one of the oldest cycling tracks in the world and was used for home games of Crystal Palace between 1914 and 1918 during World War II. The venue was originally named the London County Grounds and was the home to the London County Cycling and Athletic Club. Crystal Palace was forced by the Admiralty to leave Crystal Palace Football Stadium because it was needed for training purposes during the war, and that's how the club ended up at Herne Hill before moving to "The Nest."

2. Croydon Common Athletic Ground, generally known as "The Nest" by residents, was a soccer venue in Selhurst, South London. The ground's original tenant was a club named Croydon Common FC from 1908 to 1917. Crystal Palace used it as their home ground from 1918 to 1924. It was subleased from the London, Brighton, and South Coast Railway, who in turn had leased it from the owners, the Ecclesiastical Commissioners for England. The ground held approximately 20,000 supporters at the time.

3. The original Crystal Palace was a cast-iron and plate-glass structure located in Hyde Park, London. It was built to host the Great Exhibition of 1851, which took place from May 1 to October 15 and featured over 14,000 exhibitors from around the world. The exhibition presented examples of

technology that were developed during the Industrial Revolution. The building was 1,851 feet long, with an interior height being 128 feet making it three times the size of London's famous St Paul's Cathedral. Interior lights weren't needed due to the clear glass walls and ceilings.

4. Selhurst Park sits in Selhurst in the London Borough of Croydon. The stadium was designed by Archibald Leitch of Scotland and opened in 1924. It was used for the 1948 Summer Olympics and was also shared by fellow professional soccer clubs Charlton Athletic from 1985 to 1991 and Wimbledon FC from 1991 to 2003. The site used to be a brickfield and the club bought it from the London, Brighton, and South Coast Railway Company. The stadium was renovated in 1983, 1995, 2013, and 2014 and then expanded in 1969 and again in 1994.

5. Although the current capacity at the all-seat Selhurst Park is just over 26,000, it used to hold many more fans for soccer. The record attendance at the venue was in 1979 when 51,801 showed up to see Palace beat Burnley FC 2-0 to clinch the Second Division championship. The ground also holds the record for a fourth-tier game at 37,774 in 1961 when the Eagles played local rivals Millwall FC. In addition, Selhurst Park held the lowest recorded official attendance for a Premier League game when just 3,039 fans showed up for a match between Wimbledon and Everton on Jan. 26, 1993.

6. Starting in 1939, when World War II broke out and the Football League was placed on hold, the club played in

several competitions including the South Regional League, London League, and Football League South. The Football League then resumed action in the 1946-47 season.

7. Soon after Malcolm Allison became manager in 1973, the club's nickname was changed to the Eagles in honor of Portuguese club Benfica. Until 1973, Crystal Palace's kit colors were typically claret and blue, similar to Aston Villa, because the club had donated kits. The colors were then changed to red and blue vertical stripes in honor of FC Barcelona and are still worn today. The original amateur Crystal Palace club wore blue and white hooped shirts with blue shorts. In 1938, the team wore white shirts and black shorts until returning to claret and blue in 1949. The club has tried several other colors such as yellow and an all-white strip.

8. The club's initials were embroidered onto players' shirts in 1935-36 but a crest featuring the façade of the Crystal Palace didn't appear until the late 1940s, which lasted until 1955. A badge with the club's initials and nickname, "THE GLAZIERS," was created in 1972. However, a new badge featuring an eagle holding a soccer ball was introduced in 1973 and remained until 1987 when the eagle and Crystal Palace building were both featured on the badge. From mid-2010 to 2020, the club's mascot was an American bald eagle named Kayla. The bird flew from one end of the stadium to the other at every home game but sadly passed away in June 2020.

9. The side's only UEFA-sanctioned European competition so far, has been a spot in the 1998 UEFA Intertoto Cup. Palace played Samsunspor of Turkey in the third round and was beaten 2-0 in both the home and away legs to lose 4-0 on aggregate. The Intertoto Cup was a summer competition for European clubs that ran from 1961-62 to 2008.

10. Crystal Palace Football Club Women was originally formed in 1992 as Crystal Palace Ladies Football Club. The team competed in the FA Women's Championship in 2020-21 and like the men's side is also nicknamed the Eagles. The club is affiliated with Crystal Palace FC and plays its home matches at Hayes Lane in Bromley, which has a capacity of 5,000.

CHAPTER 3:

THE CAPTAIN CLASS

QUIZ TIME!

1. Who captained Palace to promotion to the Premier League in 2012-13?

   a. Jonathan Parr
   b. Mile Jedinak
   c. Yannick Bolasie
   d. Owen Garvan

2. George Woodger was the first full-time captain of the Crystal Palace professional team.

   a. True
   b. False

3. Who did Luka Milivojević replace as full-time captain?

   a. Christian Benteke
   b. Joel Ward
   c. Scott Dann
   d. Jason Puncheon

4. Gareth Southgate captained the Eagles to victory in which domestic competition?

    a. First Division championship
    b. FA Charity Shield
    c. Full Members Cup
    d. Second Division championship

5. Which club did Shaun Derry captain in between his two spells with Palace?

    a. Sheffield United
    b. Notts County FC
    c. Leeds United
    d. Portsmouth FC

6. How many times did Harry Hanger captain the side to the London Challenge Cup final?

    a. 0
    b. 2
    c. 4
    d. 6

7. Tony Popovic was the first team captain born in Australia.

    a. True
    b. False

8. Who captained the side to its first divisional title in the Southern League?

    a. Dick Roberts
    b. Archie Needham

c. Ted Birnie

d. Wilf Innerd

9. Which club did Paddy McCarthy captain before he joined the Eagles?

   a. Oldham Athletic

   b. Leicester City FC

   c. Southampton FC

   d. Manchester City FC

10. Who skippered Palace to their first FA Cup final?

    a. Ian Evans

    b. Jim Cannon

    c. Geoff Thomas

    d. Andy Linighan

11. Jimmy McNichol was a full-time skipper for Palace and which team?

    a. Newcastle United

    b. Chelsea FC

    c. Hurlford United

    d. Brighton & Hove Albion

12. Mile Jedinak wore the armband for the Australian men's national team in 25 matches.

    a. True

    b. False

13. Who captained the Eagles in their first Anglo-Italian Cup competition?

a. Steve Kember

b. Alan Stephenson

c. Ronnie Allen

d. John Sewell

14. Jim Cannon captained the side in which 1982-83 tournament?

a. Football League Cup

b. Football League Trophy

c. Football League Group Cup

d. Full Members Cup

15. Who replaced Hayden Mullins as full-time skipper?

a. Neil Shipperley

b. Michael Hughes

c. Fitz Hall

d. Tony Popovic

16. Palace alternated the captaincy each month in the 1966-67 season.

a. True

b. False

17. Who succeeded Gary Southgate as full-time captain?

a. Dean Austin

b. Andy Roberts

c. Neil Ruddock

d. Andy Linighan

18. Which team did Mark Hudson not captain?

a. Charlton Athletic

b. Huddersfield Town FC

c. Cardiff City FC

d. Fulham FC

19. Who Captained the Eagles in the Intertoto Cup competition?

a. Roy Barry

b. Jim Cannon

c. Andy Linighan

d. Neil Ruddock

20. George Walker was the first full-time captain appointed following World War II.

a. True

b. False

QUIZ ANSWERS

1. B – Mile Jedinak

2. B – False

3. D – Jason Puncheon

4. A – First Division championship

5. C – Leeds United

6. B – 2

7. A – True

8. C – Ted Birnie

9. C – Geoff Thomas

10. B – Leicester City FC

11. D – Brighton & Hove Albion

12. A – True

13. D – John Sewell

14. C – Football League Group Cup

15. A – Neil Shipperley

16. B – False

17. B – Andy Roberts

18. D – Fulham FC

19. C – Andy Linighan

20. B – False

DID YOU KNOW?

1. The first full-time captain of the club is believed to have been defender/midfielder Ted Birnie, who joined the side for one season in 1905-06 from Newcastle United, where he was the team's skipper. He helped Palace win the Second Division of the Southern League in 1905-06 by scoring 3 goals in 29 matches in all competitions before joining Chelsea in August 1906. After his playing career ended, Birnie took up a coaching job with German club FC Mülheim before becoming a trainer with Sunderland and Rochdale and then taking over as manager of Southend United in 1922.

2. When center-half Ted Birnie joined Chelsea in 1906, Wilf Innerd took over as skipper. He joined the team from his hometown club Newcastle United in 1905 and captained Palace during their shocking FA Cup win over Newcastle in 1907. Innerd was a regular starter with the squad, until suffering a serious injury during a January 1909 FA Cup match against Wolverhampton Wanderers. Innerd left the club in 1909 for non-league Shildon Athletic after scoring 7 goals in 133 games for Palace.

3. Signing for Palace from Chelsea in March 1958 was forward John "Johnny" McNichol, who was then appointed captain to help develop the team's promising youngsters. He scored in his debut and netted 7 goals in

the remaining 12 games of the season. In October 1958, manager George Smith relieved him of the captaincy and McNichol played several positions for the team. McNichol was given the armband back and helped the side finish as Fourth Division runners-up in 1960-61 to earn the club's promotion. His pro career was ended after he suffered a fractured cheekbone and broken jaw in the 1962-63 season, and he remained with the club in an office role. McNichol played 205 games for Palace and chipped in with 15 goals.

4. Scottish defender/midfielder Jim Cannon began his pro career with Palace after spending his youth at Selhurst Park. He was signed as an apprentice in October 1970 by manager Bert Head. He scored in his senior debut in March 1973 and went on to make a record 660 appearances for the club, scoring 35 goals. He remained until 1988 when he joined Croydon FC after spending the previous 10 years as Palace skipper. Cannon helped the club earn promotion from the Third to Second Division in 1976-77 and to the Second Division title in 1978-79. The side was relegated from the top tier two years later. In 2005, Cannon returned to Palace in the hospitality department. He was voted to the club's Centenary XI and placed second in voting as the team's Player of the Century behind Ian Wright.

5. Captaining Palace in the 1989-90 FA Cup final was English international midfielder Geoff Thomas. After playing non-league football as a teenager, he left his job as an electrician and took a pay cut to sign with Rochdale in

1982. He arrived at Selhurst Park from Crewe Alexandra in June 1987 for a reported fee of £50,000. Thomas quickly became a fan favorite and was voted the team's Player of the Year for 1990-91 and 1991-92. He also helped the squad earn promotion to the top flight during his second season. In 1990-91, the team finished third in the First Division but was relegated from the top tier in 1992-93. Thomas then joined Wolverhampton Wanderers for a reported fee of £800,000 after scoring 35 times in 249 Palace outings.

6. Current England men's national team manager Gareth Southgate also graduated from the youth system with Palace. He played with the senior side from 1988 to 1995, starting as a right-back and then moving to central midfield. He was captain of the side in 1993-94 when it won the First Division title to earn promotion to the Premier League after being relegated from the top tier the year before. However, the team was relegated again in 1994-95 after just one season in the Premier League and Southgate joined Aston Villa for a fee of £2.5 million after 152 appearances for Palace.

7. Australian international center-back Tony Popovic signed for Palace on a free transfer in August 2001 from Sanfrecce Hiroshima in Japan, where he joined in 1997 after starting his career in his homeland. Popovic became an integral part of the Eagles defense and was eventually given the captain's armband. He played 144 times for the side but decided not to accept the club's offer of a new

contract when his deal expired at the end of June 2006. Popovic then joined Al-Arabi in Qatar and later became an assistant manager with Palace in 2011-12 when Dougie Freedman was the boss. As a player, he helped the side win the 2003-04 playoffs to earn promotion to the Premier League and was managing Melbourne victory in 2021.

8. Another Australian international captain with Palace was Mile Jedinak who arrived from Turkish side Gençlerbirliği in 2011. He quickly became a fan favorite and was appointed skipper in 2012-13 when regular skipper Paddy McCarthy was injured. Jedinak scored an 89th-minute winner on the final day of the campaign to beat Peterborough United and secure a playoff place for the team. He then led the squad to the promotion to the Premier League by winning the playoffs and was voted the club's Player of the Season. Jedinak was named Asian International Footballer of the Year for 2014 and his free-kick goal against Liverpool was voted Palace's Goal of the Season for 2014. In addition, Palace reached the 2015-156 FA Cup final. Before the 2016-17 Premier League season kicked off Jedinak resigned the captaincy and Scott Dann took over and he left for Aston Villa after close to 200 games with the Eagles.

9. Midfielder Hayden Mullins joined the Eagles as a trainee in August 1996 and made his senior debut as a 19-year-old in July 1998. He immediately established himself as a regular starter and played 45 times in 1998-99 while being voted the team's Player of the Year. He played 51 times in

2000-01 as Palace reached the semifinals of the League Cup but was transfer-listed in October 2000. However, he remained with the club and was appointed captain for the 2002-03 campaign by manager Trevor Francis. He guided the side to the quarterfinals of the League Cup and was voted Player of the Year again. Mullins joined West Ham United in October 2003 after scoring 20 goals in 257 games with Palace.

10. As of May 2021, the club skipper was Serbian international midfielder Luka Milivojević who arrived in January 2017 from Olympiacos of Greece. He led the side in scoring with 10 goals in 2017-18 and again in 2018-19 with 12 goals, many of them on penalty kicks. Oddly, he had never taken a penalty in a pro game before joining Palace and was successful on 9 of his first 10 attempts. In August 2019, Milivojević signed a contract extension with the club that would theoretically see him stay at Selhurst Park until 2023. As of mid-May 2021, he had appeared in 157 games and scored 28 goals.

CHAPTER 4:

AMAZING MANAGERS

QUIZ TIME!

1. Who was recognized as the club's first manager in 1905, after it turned professional?

   a. Edmund Goodman

   b. John "Jack" Robson

   c. Alex Maley

   d. Fred Mavin

2. The club was managed by a committee between 1945 and 1949.

   a. True

   b. False

3. Who was the club's first caretaker-manager born outside of the British Isles?

   a. Frank de Boer

   b. Attilio Lombardo

   c. Gerard Houllier

   d. Tony Pulis

4. Which club did Bert Head leave to join Palace?

   a. Swansea City FC
   b. Crawley Town FC
   c. Preston North End
   d. Bury FC

5. Who managed the side during its first season in the Football League?

   a. Jack Tresadern
   b. Tom Bromilow
   c. Edmund Goodman
   d. Fred Mavin

6. Terry Venables ended his first spell with Palace to manage which club?

   a. Sunderland AFC
   b. Nottingham Forest FC
   c. Queens Park Rangers
   d. Leicester City FC

7. Alex Maley managed the club to its first divisional title in the Southern League.

   a. True
   b. False

8. Which manager led the side in its first Premier League campaign?

   a. Dave Basset
   b. Terry Venables

c. Ron Noades

d. Steve Coppell

9. How many stints did Alan Smith serve as Palace's full-time manager?

a. 3

b. 5

c. 2

d. 1

10. Ian Holloway led the Eagles to victory in what tournament in 2012-13?

a. Football League Trophy

b. Championship League playoffs

c. Full Members Cup

d. Football League Group Cup

11. Which manager took Palace to the 2015-16 FA Cup final?

a. Sam Allardyce

b. Alan Pardew

c. Frank de Boer

d. Keith Millen

12. Attilio Lombardo was made caretaker player-manager in 1998.

a. True

b. False

13. How many stints did Steve Coppell have as a full-time manager of the team?

a. 1

b. 2

c. 4

d. 5

14. From which club did Frank de Boer join Palace?

 a. Inter Milan

 b. Juventus

 c. Paris Saint-Germain

 d. FC Barcelona

15. Who succeeded Steve Kember as manager in 2003?

 a. Peter Taylor

 b. Neil Warnock

 c. Trevor Francis

 d. Iain Dowie

16. Alan Mullery managed the side to its first FA Cup final.

 a. True

 b. False

17. Who did Ian Holloway succeed as manager?

 a. George Burley

 b. Dougie Freedman

 c. Tony Pulis

 d. Neil Warnock

18. Cyril Spiers left Palace to manage what club?

 a. Portsmouth FC

 b. Blackburn Rovers

c. Exeter City FC

d. Norwich City FC

19. Who was the first Palace manager to win the Premier League Manager of the Season Award?

a. Iain Dowie

b. Alan Pardew

c. Roy Hodgson

d. Tony Pulis

20. Roy Hodgson was appointed manager following Frank de Boer's dismissal.

a. True

b. False

QUIZ ANSWERS

1. B – John "Jack" Robson

2. B – False

3. B – Attilio Lombardo

4. D – Bury FC

5. C – Edmund Goodman

6. C – Queens Park Rangers

7. B – False

8. D – Steve Coppell

9. C – 2

10. B – 2012-13 Championship League playoffs

11. B – Alan Pardew

12. A – True

13. C – 4

14. A – Inter Milan

15. D – Iain Dowie

16. B – False

17. B – Dougie Freedman

18. C – Exeter City FC

19. D – Tony Pulis

20. A – True

DID YOU KNOW?

1. Crystal Palace has appointed approximately 50 different managers and caretaker-managers. The first full-time manager was John "Jack" Robson from 1905 to 1907 and the most recent was Roy Hodgson, who was appointed in September 2017 and left when his contract expired after the 2020-21 campaign. The longest-serving manager has been Edmund Goodman between 1907 and 1925 with over 600 official competitive games in charge, excluding wartime competition.

2. Several men have had more than one stint as Palace boss or caretaker-manager over the years. Malcolm Allison, Tom Bromilow, Arthur Rowe, Alan Smith, Terry Venables, and Neil Warnock each served two stints with the club. Keith Millen had three short stints as caretaker and Steve Kember had four relatively short spells. Steve Coppell held the position on four different occasions between 1984 and 2000.

3. Each of the club's managers from 1905 to 1998 was British, and all of them were English except for Alex Maley of Scotland between 1925 and 1927. The first non-British manager was former Palace player Attilio Lombardo, who held the job for a brief spell in 1998 as caretaker player-manager. The only other manager to hail from outside the British Isles (England, Scotland, Wales, Northern Ireland,

Republic of Ireland) was Dutchman Frank de Boer, who was in charge for just a handful of games in 2017.

4. The Eagles have had one manager from Wales, Tony Pulis, who held the job between 2013 and 2014. Kit Symons was caretaker in 2003 and played internationally for Wales but was born in Basingstoke, England. Alex Maley (1925-1927), George Burley (20101-11), and Dougie Freedman (2010-11) were all born in Scotland, while caretaker Curtis Fleming (2012), who played internationally for the Republic of Ireland, was born in Manchester, England.

5. John "Jack" Robson of England was the full-time secretary-manager of Middlesbrough from 1899 to 1905 before joining Palace. He took Middlesbrough from being an amateur club in the Northern League to a professional team in the First Division of the English Football League. With Palace, Robson is recognized as being the club's first secretary-manager and he guided the side to a huge FA Cup shocker when the squad beat Newcastle United away in 1907. He also won the Southern League's Second Division title in 1905-06. Robson left in 1907 to take over at Brighton & Hove Albion.

6. Steve Coppell has arguably been the most successful manager of the Eagles because he won the Second Division playoffs in 1988-89, the Full Members' Cup in 1990-91, and the First Division playoffs in 1996-97. He also led the side to the 1989-90 FA Cup final and to a third-place finish in the top-flight First Division in 1990-91, the

club's highest finish ever. The former English international winger was in charge at Selhurst Park for 13 years in total over four different stints between 1984 and 2000 to rank as the club's second longest-serving manager. In 2005, Coppell was voted as the manager for the club's Centenary XI.

7. One of the shortest English Premier League managerial stints in history belonged to former Dutch international defender Frank de Boer, who lasted just 77 days with the club. De Boer was announced as the team's manager on June 26, 2017, to replace Sam Allardyce after signing a three-year contract. However, he was fired 10 weeks after Palace lost their first four league matches of the season and failed to score a single goal. It was the worst start for a top-flight English club in 93 years. He managed the side for just five games with the only victory being against Ipswich Town in a League Cup contest. De Boer was replaced by Roy Hodgson.

8. The only Palace manager to win a Manager of the Year Award was Tony Pulis for his work in 2013-14. He officially took the job on Nov. 23, 2013, to take over from Ian Holloway after the season had started and he signed a 2½-year contract. He was named the Premier League's Manager of the Month for April 2014 and took the yearly honor after guiding the team to an 11th-place finish with 45 points. Pulis then left the club by mutual consent before the 2014-15 campaign kicked off. In November 2016, he was ordered by a court to pay the club £3.7

million for fraudulent misrepresentation in a dispute over a £2 million bonus paid to him before departing.

9. After managing Wimbledon, Watford, and Sheffield United, Dave Bassett accepted an offer to become manager of Second Division Palace in June 1984. However, he changed his mind 72 hours later and refused to sign the contract. Bassett then returned to Wimbledon and claimed he didn't believe he'd be a good fit at Selhurst Park. However, 12 years later, Bassett had another change of mind and took over as Palace manager in early February 1996 when the side was in the second-tier First Division. The team finished the campaign in third place but lost the playoff final in extra time 2-1 to Leicester City. Bassett left in March 1997 to take over at Nottingham Forest.

10. Italian international midfielder Attilio Lombardo arrived at Selhurst Park in 1997 and scored in his debut but the team was relegated from the Premier League at the end of the 1997-98 season. In early 1998, Mark Goldberg assumed control of the club while manager Steve Coppell took over as the director of football. With no manager in place, Lombardo made club history by taking over as player-manager on a caretaker basis in mid-March to become the club's first boss to hail from outside the British Isles. He held the position until the end of the season when Terry Venables took over as full-time manager. Lombardo remained as a player until leaving in January 1999 for S.S. Lazio with 10 goals in 49 appearances under his belt.

CHAPTER 5:

GOALTENDING GREATS

QUIZ TIME!

1. Which keeper made the most appearances for the club?

   a. Nigel Martyn
   b. John Jackson
   c. Joshua Johnson
   d. Julián Speroni

2. Perry Suckling played in the Eagles first Premier League match.

   a. True
   b. False

3. Which club did Wayne Hennessey leave to join Crystal Palace?

   a. Bristol City FC
   b. Manchester City FC
   c. Stockport County FC
   d. Wolverhampton Wanderers

4. Who appeared in 28 matches in the 2002-03 domestic league?

   a. Aleksandrs Kolinko
   b. Cédric Berthelin
   c. Matt Clarke
   d. Cédric Carrasso

5. How many clean sheets did Nigel Martyn post in the 1992-93 Premier League?

   a. 5
   b. 8
   c. 11
   d. 14

6. Who played in all 38 games in the 1997-98 domestic league season?

   a. Stuart Taylor
   b. Aleksandrs Kolinko
   c. Rhys Wilmot
   d. Kevin Miller

7. Joshua Johnson made five appearances for the English men's national team.

   a. True
   b. False

8. How many appearances did John Jackson make in all competitions with the team?

   a. 448
   b. 415

c. 404

d. 388

9. Who backed up Cédric Berthelin in 15 matches in the 2003-04 domestic league?

a. Nico Vaesen

b. Scott Flinders

c. Thomas Myhre

d. Nikolaos Michopoulos

10. Which club did Vicente Guaita join Palace from?

a. Getafe CF

b. RCD Espanyol

c. Valencia CF

d. Recreativo de Huelva

11. How many clean sheets did Julián Speroni keep in the 2011-12 Championship League?

a. 16

b. 14

c. 10

d. 7

12. Vic Rouse played his entire professional career with Crystal Palace.

a. True

b. False

13. How many appearances did Nigel Martyn make in all competitions with Crystal Palace?

a. 435

b. 411

c. 349

d. 322

14. Who backed up Vicente Guaita in 18 matches in the 2018-19 domestic league?

    a. Steve Mandanda

    b. Wayne Hennessey

    c. Lucas Perri

    d. Stephen Henderson

15. Which keeper made only one appearance in the 2010-11 domestic league?

    a. Darryl Flahavan

    b. Ross Fitzsimons

    c. David Wilkinson

    d. Lewis Price

16. Gábor Király kept 15 clean sheets in the 2005-06 Championship League.

    a. True

    b. False

17. How many appearances did Julián Speroni make for the side in all competitions?

    a. 431

    b. 405

    c. 396

    d. 368

18. Which keeper appeared in 32 matches in the 2004-05 domestic league?

    a. Matt Clarke

    b. Iain Turner

    c. Gábor Király

    d. Scott Flinders

19. George Wood left Crystal Palace to join what club?

    a. West Ham United

    b. Cardiff City FC

    c. Fulham FC

    d. Hereford United

20. Steve Mandanda played only 9 career league games with the Eagles.

    a. True

    b. False

QUIZ ANSWERS

1. D – Julián Speroni

2. B – False

3. D – Wolverhampton Wanderers

4. A – Aleksandrs Kolinko

5. C – 11

6. D – Kevin Miller

7. B – False

8. D – 388

9. C – Thomas Myhre

10. A – Getafe CF

11. A – 16

12. B – False

13. C – 349

14. B – Wayne Hennessey

15. D – Lewis Price

16. A – True

17. B – 405

18. C – Gábor Király

19. B – Cardiff City FC

20. A – True

DID YOU KNOW?

1. Crystal Palace goalkeepers who have been voted the club's Player of the Year since the award was first given out in 1972 are: 1981-82, Paul Barron; 1985-86, George Wood; 2007-08, Julián Speroni; 2008-09, Julián Speroni; 2009-10, Julián Speroni; and 2013-14, Julián Speroni.

2. Joshua "Joe" Johnson was one of the club's earliest goalkeeping stars after joining the team from Plymouth Argyle in 1907. Johnson spent almost eight years with the club and played 295 times before World War I interrupted his career in 1919, 276 of these matches were in league play. When the war ended, Johnson left the Southern League to sign with Second Division club Nottingham Forest.

3. After playing for his hometown team, Prudhoe Town, Billy Callender joined Palace in 1923 as the understudy to Jack Alderson and appeared in just two matches in his first two seasons. He became the regular starter in 1925-26 and played for the Football League representative the next season. Callender racked up 225 appearances for the Eagles but sadly took his own life in July 1932 at the age of 29. He was distressed over the death of his fiancée from polio and was found hanging in the squad's dressing room following a training session.

4. Coming up through Palace's junior ranks was John Jackson, who was also playing with the England youth

team. He was brought in as backup to Bill Glazier and battled Tony Millington for the top job when Glazier joined Coventry City in 1964. He went on to play 222 straight games with the team and helped it earn promotion to the top flight for the first time by finishing as Second Division runners-up in 1968-69. After Palace was relegated in 1973, Jackson joined Leyton Orient. Nicknamed "Stonewall," Jackson played 388 times for the Eagles, the second-most by a goalkeeper.

5. Incredibly, John Burridge played with approximately 30 different clubs during his career from 1969 to 1997. The journeyman arrived at Selhurst Park in 1978 from Aston Villa when he was signed by manager Terry Venables. He stayed for two-and-a-half seasons before joining Venables at Queens Park Rangers. Burridge played close to 800 games in British leagues and many more at the non-league level. Nicknamed "Budgie," just like Palace's Johnny Byrne, he later became a goalkeeping coach in the United Arab Emirates. The colorful Burridge played 102 times with the Eagles and was popular with the fans, especially after helping the team win the Second Division in 1978-79 to reach the top flight.

6. Paul Barron was a physical education instructor before trying his hand at pro soccer and he played with non-league teams before signing with Plymouth Argyle in July 1976. He joined Arsenal two years later as cover for Pat Jennings and moved to Palace in 1980 along with forward Clive Allen while defender Kenny Sansom joined Arsenal

in the deal. Barron took over the top job from John Burridge, but the team was relegated from the top flight after his first season. He was voted the team's Player of the Year for 1981-82 but left to join West Bromwich Albion at the end of the campaign. Barron became a goalkeeping coach after his playing career and later managed the Las Vegas Mobsters in America.

7. Scottish international George Wood began his career with East Stirling and once scored from his own penalty area in 1971. He joined Palace in 1983 as the number-one keeper from Arsenal and went on to make 221 appearances before joining Cardiff City in January 1998. He was voted the side's Player of the Year for 1985-1986 and played 100 consecutive league outings, which began with his Palace debut. After hanging up his boots, Wood became a goalkeeping coach and returned to Selhurst Park in that capacity in 2012.

8. After starting out as a midfielder, Nigel Martyn tried goalkeeping as a 17-year-old and played with several amateur sides while working in a plastics factory and for a coal merchant. He began his pro career with Bristol Rovers in 1987 and went on to play 23 times with England's senior side. He was transferred to Palace for a fee of £1 million in 1989, becoming the first keeper in English football to cost that much. Martyn remained with the club for seven seasons and appeared in 349 games, including the 1990 FA Cup final and the replay, as well as the 1990-91 Full Members' Cup, which Palace won. Martyn joined Leeds

United in 1996 for a new record for a goalkeeper of £2.25 million.

9. Julián Speroni of Argentina has played the most games for the Eagles as a goalkeeper at 405. He was voted the team's Player of the Year a record four times as he took the award home in 2007-08, 2008-09, 2009-10, and 2013-14. He started his career in his homeland with Platense before playing three seasons in the Scottish Premier League with Dundee. He joined newly promoted Premier League side Palace in 2004 for a reported £750,000 and backed up Gábor Király until he left in 2007. Speroni flourished with the team and helped it win the second-tier Championship League playoffs in 2012-13 and reach the 2015-16 FA Cup final. He stayed with the side until hanging up his boots and gloves in 2019.

10. Welsh international Wayne Hennessey left Wolverhampton Wanderers for the Eagles in January 2014 but didn't make his debut until the side's final contest of the Premier League season on May 11 because Julián Speroni was the number-one keeper. He became a regular in 2015-16 and helped the side reach the FA Cup final but gave way to fellow keeper Vicente Guaita for most of the 2018-19 campaign. Hennessey played just five times in 2019-20 and then suffered an injury in October 2020 that kept him out of action until February 2021. He's played 95 times for Wales. He is the cousin of former Welsh international player Terry Hennessey. He was still with the club in May 2021 and had made 132 appearances.

CHAPTER 6:

DARING DEFENDERS

QUIZ TIME!

1. Which player made the most appearances in all competitions for the team?

    a. Jim Cannon
    b. Paul Hinshelwood
    c. Terry Long
    d. Bob Greener

2. Eric Young played in all 42 games in the 1992-93 Premier League season.

    a. True
    b. False

3. How many goals did Jamie Smith score in the 2001-02 domestic league?

    a. 4
    b. 1
    c. 7
    d. 3

4. Which player netted 3 goals in the 2019-20 Premier League?

   a. Cheikhou Kouyaté

   b. Scott Dann

   c. Martin Kelly

   d. Patrick van Aanholt

5. Billy Gilbert left Crystal Palace to join which club?

   a. Southampton FC

   b. Newcastle United

   c. Millwall FC

   d. Portsmouth FC

6. Who won the club's Player of the Year award in 2018-19?

   a. Patrick van Aanholt

   b. James Tomkins

   c. Aaron Wan-Bissaka

   d. Mamadou Sakho

7. Terry Long played his entire professional career with the Eagles.

   a. True

   b. False

8. How many appearances did Paul Hinshelwood make in all competitions for Palace?

   a. 319

   b. 356

   c. 411

   d. 447

9. Who led the club with nine yellow cards in all competitions in 2015-16?

   a. Pape Souaré

   b. Scott Dann

   c. Joel Ward

   d. Damien Delaney

10. How many goals did Jimmy Wilde score in all competitions with the side?

   a. 0

   b. 1

   c. 6

   d. 35

11. Who was voted the club's Player of the Year in 1971-72?

   a. Tony Taylor

   b. Derek Jeffries

   c. Kenny Sansom

   d. John McCormick

12. Mark Kennedy tallied 10 assists in the 2006-07 domestic league season.

   a. True

   b. False

13. How many appearances did Terry Long make in all competitions with Palace?

   a. 459

   b. 480

c. 499

d. 531

14. Who was shown eight yellow cards in the 2016-17 Premier League?

    a. Timothy Fosu-Mensah

    b. Martin Kelly

    c. James Tomkins

    d. Joel Ward

15. How many goals did Darren Ward tally in all competitions in 2005-06?

    a. 2

    b. 5

    c. 6

    d. 9

16. Harry Collyer scored just 1 goal in 281 appearances with the squad.

    a. True

    b. False

17. Which player made 43 appearances in the 2009-10 Championship League?

    a. Danny Butterfield

    b. Clint Hill

    c. José Fonte

    d. Claude Davis

18. How many appearances did Jim Cannon make in all competitions with the team?

a. 612

b. 640

c. 660

d. 672

19. Who appeared in 48 games in all competitions in 2005-06?

a. Fitz Hall

b. Darren Ward

c. Emmerson Boyce

d. Mark Hudson

20. Fan Zhiyi made 106 appearances for the Chinese men's national team.

a. True

b. False

QUIZ ANSWERS

1. A – Jim Cannon

2. B – False

3. A – 4

4. D – Patrick van Aanholt

5. D – Portsmouth FC

6. C – Aaron Wan-Bissaka

7. A – True

8. A – 319

9. B – Scott Dann

10. C – 6

11. D – John McCormick

12. B – False

13. B – 480

14. C – James Tomkins

15. C – 6

16. A – True

17. B – Clint Hill

18. C – 660

19. C – Emmerson Boyce

20. A – True

DID YOU KNOW?

1. Crystal Palace defenders who have been voted the club's Player of the Year since the award was first given out in 1972 are: 1971-72, John McCormick; 1972-73, Tony Taylor; 1974-75, Derek Jeffries; 1976-77, Kenny Sansom; 1977-78, Jim Cannon; 1978-79, Kenny Sansom; 1979-80, Paul Hinshelwood; 1980-81, Paul Hinshelwood; 1983-84, Billy Gilbert; 1984-85, Jim Cannon; 1986-87, Jim Cannon; 1992-93, Andy Thorn; 1993-94, Chris Coleman; 1994-95, Richard Shaw; 1997-98, Marc Edworthy; 1999-2000, Andy Linighan; 2000-01, Fan Zhiyi; 2005-06, Emmerson Boyce; 2006-07, Leon Cort; 2010-11, Nathaniel Clyne; 2011-12, Jonathan Parr; 2014-15, Scott Dann; and 2018-19, Aaron Wan-Bissaka.

2. Harry Collyer joined Palace in 1906, just in time for the team's second pro season and its first in the Southern League First Division after winning the second tier the previous year. He started out as a left-back but moved to right-back and established himself on the squad. Collyer remained at Palace until the outbreak of World War I in 1915 and in 1912 he became the first club player to earn a testimonial match. He played in 263 Southern League matches and another 18 in the FA Cup for a total of 281. He scored just once. When the war broke out, Collyer was the longest-serving player with the side and held the mark until Albert Harry passed him in the 1930s.

3. James "Jimmy" Hughes signed for Liverpool in June 1904 after playing for several amateur sides. However, he was just a part-time player with the Reds and played just 15 official competitive contests with the club over five seasons, never playing more than five times on a single campaign. He left Liverpool in 1909 for Palace and went on to score 15 times in 209 outings in the Southern League from 1909 until 1920. However, the league was placed on hold when World War I broke out in 1915, resuming in 1919. Hughes served as club captain for part of his career and joined non-league Chatham in 1920 due to an injury just before Palace entered the Football League.

4. Spending his entire pro career with Palace between 1928 and 1938 was Jimmy Wilde, the captain of the club for six seasons. He signed with the side in November after leaving the Army, where he had served with the Royal Tank Corps. He soon became a regular starter and was a member of Palace squads that finished as runners-up in the Third Division South in 1928-29 and 1930-31. Wilde lost his starting position in 1936 and played just three more times with the team before hanging up his boots and helping as a coach. He played nearly 300 games with the squad and contributed six goals.

5. After playing with amateur club Sutton United, Len Choules signed as a pro with Palace in May 1951 but didn't make his debut until April 1953. He went on to appear in 280 games and chipped in with 3 goals while playing wherever he was needed on the park as well as

his usual right-back position. He helped the team earn promotion from the Fourth Division in season 1960-61 by finishing as runners-up. Choules received two testimonials from the club before leaving for non-league side Romford on a free transfer in 1962 and in 1954 he was selected to an FA XI to play against Oxford University.

6. Terry Long held the club record for appearances at 480 until Jim Cannon set the current mark at 660. Long played his entire career with the team, from May 1955 to 1970. He joined the side when it was in the Third Division South and then played in the fourth, third, and second tiers of the league during his time at Selhurst Park. Long once played 214 consecutive games and was a part of the 1960-1961, 1963-1964, and 1968-69 promotion squads. He didn't play in the First Division in 1969-70 when the club reached the top flight for the first time, though. That means that Long played for the team in four different divisions of the Football League, but not in the top tier. After retiring, he remained with the club as a coach and later served as assistant manager to Bert Head.

7. Former England schoolboy player Kenny Sansom was scouted by Arsenal, Queens Park Rangers, and Tottenham Hotspur but decided to join the youth team at Palace. He captained the junior team to the 1976-77 FA Youth Cup title, and he also wore the armband for the England youth team. In addition, Sansom was voted the Eagles' Player of the Year in his first season. He helped the team win the 1978-79 Second Division to reach the top tier of the

Football League for the second time. Arsenal offered £1 million for Sansom in the summer of 1980, with striker Clive Allen joining Palace in the transaction. Sansom then joined Arsenal after 197 appearances with Palace and went on to become the second-most-capped England national team full-back with 86 appearances.

8. Manager Arthur Rowe was impressed by Paul Hinshelwood and his brother Martin when they played in the London FA Schools Cup final, and they were both invited for trials with Palace. They were taken on as apprentices, with Paul being a striker at the time. He then switched to right-back in November 1976 and helped the side earn promotion in 1976-77 and win the Second Division in 1978-79 to reach the top flight. Palace spent two years in the top tier and Hinshelwood was voted the team's Player of the Year both seasons. He left the club in 1983 for Oxford United after playing 319 games and scoring 28 goals. Hinshelwood's father Wally was a pro soccer player in the 1950s and '60s and brother Martin's career was cut short due to injury. In 2005, Paul was named in the club's Centenary XI.

9. Emmerson Boyce played internationally for Barbados even though he was born in Aylesbury, England. He left Luton Town for Crystal Palace in July 2004 on a free transfer and signed a two-year contract. Boyce quickly became the side's first choice right-back but they were relegated from the Premier League on the final day of the season after drawing Charlton Athletic. Palace missed out

on promotion in 2005-06 because they were beaten by Watford in the playoff semifinals, Boyce was voted the team's Player of the Year. With a year to go on his contract, Boyce rejected a new contract because he wanted to return to the Premier League. He was sold to Wigan Athletic in August 2006 after 77 games with Palace.

10. English international Nathaniel Clyne spent his youth days with Palace and made his first-team debut in October 2008, signing a three-year professional contract two days later. In February 2010, he was offered a move to Premier League side Wolverhampton Wanderers but turned it down. In the 2010-11 campaign, Clyne was the youngest player in the Football League to play every single match and was voted the team's Player of the Year. After 137 games, Clyne signed with Liverpool in July 2012 but returned to Selhurst Park in October 2020 and had played a further 14 times as of May 2021.

CHAPTER 7:

MAESTROS OF THE MIDFIELD

QUIZ TIME!

1. Who played the most games for the Eagles?

    a. Simon Rodger
    b. David Payne
    c. Bill Turner
    d. Albert Harry

2. James McArthur played all 38 games in the 2019-20 Premier League.

    a. True
    b. False

3. How many goals did Ben Watson score in all competitions in 2007-08?

    a. 2
    b. 5
    c. 7
    d. 12

4. Who won the club's Player of the Year award in 1973-74?

   a. Bobby Kellard
   b. Don Rogers
   c. Peter Taylor
   d. Nick Chatterton

5. Phil Barber left Palace to join which club?

   a. Millwall FC
   b. Portsmouth FC
   c. Bristol City FC
   d. Sunderland AFC

6. Who recorded 7 assists in the 20011-12 domestic league?

   a. Mile Jedinak
   b. David Wright
   c. Owen Garvan
   d. Darren Ambrose

7. Simon Rodger made three appearances for the English men's national team.

   a. True
   b. False

8. How many appearances did David Payne make in all competitions?

   a. 380
   b. 346
   c. 330
   d. 326

9. Who scored 5 goals in the 2015-16 domestic league?

   a. Yohan Cabaye

   b. Jordan Mutch

   c. Joe Ledley

   d. James McArthur

10. Steve Kember joined which club after his first stint with the Eagles ended?

    a. San Jose Earthquakes

    b. Chelsea FC

    c. Liverpool FC

    d. VfL Wolfsburg

11. Who made 49 appearances in all competitions in 2005-06?

    a. Ben Watson

    b. Tom Soares

    c. Mikele Leigertwood

    d. Aki Riihilahti

12. Bill Turner scored 37 goals in all competitions with Palace.

    a. True

    b. False

13. Who netted 8 goals in the 2009-10 Championship League?

    a. Nick Carle

    b. Victor Mosses

    c. Shaun Derry

    d. Neil Danns

14. How many appearances did Simon Rodger make in all competitions for Palace?

    a. 289
    b. 328
    c. 344
    d. 367

15. Which player was shown eight yellow cards in the 2017-18 domestic league?

    a. Jeffrey Schlupp
    b. Yohan Cabaye
    c. Ruben Loftus-Cheek
    d. Luka Milivojević

16. Shaun Derry was the only Palace player to be shown a red card in the 2009-10 Championship League.

    a. True
    b. False

17. Who won the club's 2012-13 Player of the Year award?

    a. Jonny Williams
    b. Kagisho Dikgacoi
    c. Mile Jedinak
    d. Owen Garvan

18. How many appearances did Albert Harry Make in all competitions?

    a. 392
    b. 418

c. 440

d. 459

19. Which year did Ben Watson win the club's Young Player of the Year award?

   a. 2007

   b. 2006

   c. 2005

   d. 2004

20. Nick Chatterton played his entire professional career with the Eagles.

   a. True

   b. False

QUIZ ANSWERS

1. D – Albert Harry
2. B – False
3. C – 7
4. C – Peter Taylor
5. A – Millwall FC
6. D – Darren Ambrose
7. B – False
8. D – 326
9. A – Yohan Cabaye
10. B – Chelsea FC
11. B – Tom Soares
12. A – True
13. D – Neil Danns
14. B – 328
15. D – Luka Milivojević
16. B – False
17. C – Mile Jedinak
18. C – 440
19. B – 2006
20. B – False

DID YOU KNOW?

1. Crystal Palace midfielders who have been voted the club's Player of the Year since the award was first given out in 1972 are as follows: 1973-74, Peter Taylor; 1975-76, Peter Taylor; 1982-83, Jerry Murphy; 1987-88, Geoff Thomas; 1990-91, Geoff Thomas; 1991-92, Eddie McGoldrick; 1995-96, Andy Roberts; 1996-97, David Hopkin; 1998-99, Hayden Mullins; 2002-03, Hayden Mullins; 2012-13, Mile Jedinak.

2. Scoring 37 times in 302 appearances for Palace between 1925 and 1936 was William "Billy" Turner. He arrived from non-league Bromsgrove Rovers in May and played every position for the club at least once other than goalkeeper and center-back. The England schoolboy international was well known for this versatility and commitment to the team and earned the nickname "Rubber." He played his entire Palace career in the Third Division South before heading back to non-league football in June 1936 when he signed for Worcester City where he finished his playing career.

3. Peter Taylor managed the Eagles between 2006 and 2007 and played with the team between 1973 and 1976. He joined Palace in October 1973 from Southend United for a reported £110,000 and was voted the team's Player of the Year in his first campaign even though it was relegated. He was named Player of the Year again for 1975-76 and

helped the club reach the FA Cup semifinals by scoring twice in their quarterfinal victory at Chelsea. Taylor also made four appearances for England that season and became one of a few players to play for the senior England squad even though he was not playing in the top two flights of a domestic league. He signed with Tottenham Hotspur in September 1976 for a reported £400,000 fee after 39 goals in 142 Palace outings.

4. Jerry Murphy was a Republic of Ireland international who was born in England and scored 25 times in 269 outings with the Eagles. He spent time with the youth setup at Selhurst Park and helped the side win the FA Youth Cup in 1976-1977 and 1977-1978 as part of the famous "Team of the Eighties" Palace squad. He helped the club earn promotion to the top-tier First Division in 1978-79 by winning the second tier in his first full season in the side. However, they were relegated after two years in the top flight. Murphy was voted the team's Player of the Year for 1982-83 and then moved back to the top flight by joining Chelsea on a free transfer in the summer of 1985.

5. After playing for the Eagles youth side in 1980-81, Andy Gray played non-league soccer before heading back to Selhurst Park in 1984. He shared the team scoring lead with Phil Barber in 1985-86 with 11 goals while playing up front. Gray moved to midfield after the club signed Ian Wright and Mark Bright and remained with the team until joining Aston Villa in 1987. Gray returned to Palace in 1989 and scored in the FA Cup semifinals against

Liverpool to seal the team's spot in the final against Manchester United. The club finished third in the top tier the next season, 1990-91, and won the Full Members' Cup. Gray then left Palace for Tottenham Hotspur for a reported £900,000 after scoring 51 goals in 242 games. He was voted to Palace's Centenary XI in 2005.

6. After playing non-league football with Bognor Regis Town, Simon Rodger was signed by the Eagles in 1990 for a reported £1,000 and made his debut as a 20-year-old. He became a key player with the side and spent 11 seasons and 328 games at Selhurst Park. He played in the inaugural Premier League season, but the club was relegated following the campaign. He then helped the squad earn an instant return in 1993-94, which was followed by relegation in 1994-95 and another promotion in 1996-97, this time via the playoffs. Rodger spent part of 1996-97 on loan with Manchester City and Stoke City and he suffered a third relegation from the Premier League in 1997-98. After his testimonial match in 2002, Rodger was released and soon signed with Brighton & Hove Albion, where he was reunited with former Palace manager Steve Coppell.

7. South African international Kagisho Dikgacoi arrived at Selhurst Park in February 2011 on a loan deal from Fulham until the end of the 2010-11 season. He moved permanently to the Eagles in July 2011 for a reported fee of £600,000. He remained with the club until June 2014 when he penned a three-year deal with Cardiff City after rejecting a new contract with Palace. Dikgacoi played over

100 games with Palace, scoring 8 goals. He scored twice in 54 games for his homeland. He also helped Palace earn promotion to the Premier League in 2012-13 by winning the Championship League playoffs.

8. In August 2013, Jason Puncheon signed a one-year loan with Palace from Southampton and made it a permanent move in January 2014 for a reported fee of approximately £1.75 million. He helped the squad reach the 2015-16 FA Cup final against Manchester United and opened the scoring in the 78th minute of the team's 2-1 extra-time defeat. Puncheon replaced Scott Dann as captain in July 2017 but an injury in January 2018 forced him to miss the test of the season. He left the club following the 2018-19 campaign after scoring 16 times in 169 appearances when he joined Huddersfield Town. Puncheon signed with First Division side Paros in Cyprus in 2019 and was still there in 2020-21.

9. Scottish international James McArthur joined Palace from Wigan Athletic on the last day of the summer 2014 transfer window, for a reported £7 million fee and signed a three-year contract. He tore ankle ligaments in February 2016 but returned in time to play in the 2015-16 FA Cup final against Manchester United in May. McArthur was still with Palace in 2020-21 and had scored 19 goals in 226 appearances. All 215 of his league outings with the team have come in the Premier League and he also scored 4 goals in 32 appearances with Scotland.

10. After winning several individual and team awards with Leicester City, German-born Ghanaian international Jeffrey Schlupp joined Palace in January 2017 for a reported £12 million. He's helped the club keep its top-flight status since joining and was still with the Eagles as of May 2021, with 10 goals in 122 appearances. He kicked off his soccer career as a striker and plays as a left-back-or winger with Ghana. Schlupp missed a few months of the 2020-21 campaign due to injury and upon his return became the Ghanaian player with the most career appearances in the Premier League when he played his 169th game on May 8 to surpass Michael Essien's 168.

CHAPTER 8:

SENSATIONAL STRIKERS/FORWARDS

QUIZ TIME!

1. Who has played the most career games with the club?

    a. Dougie Freedman

    b. Wilfried Zaha

    c. Mark Bright

    d. Clinton Morrison

2. Michy Batshuayi scored 5 goals in 11 games while on loan from Chelsea FC in the 2018-19 Premier League.

    a. True

    b. False

3. How many goals did Eddie McGoldrick score in the 1992-93 Premier League?

    a. 3

    b. 6

    c. 8

    d. 13

4. Who scored 9 goals in all competitions in 2007-08?

   a. Sean Scannell
   b. Paul Ifill
   c. Scott Sinclair
   d. James Scowcroft

5. Which side did Mark Bright join after leaving Palace?

   a. Wes Ham United
   b. Aston Villa
   c. Sheffield Wednesday
   d. Leeds United

6. Who made 39 appearances in the 2002-03 domestic league?

   a. Julian Gray
   b. Andy Johnson
   c. Dele Adebola
   d. Wayne Routledge

7. Christian Benteke had played 39 times for the Belgian men's national team.

   a. True
   b. False

8. How many appearances did Dougie Freedman make in all competitions for Palace?

   a. 429
   b. 403
   c. 368
   d. 355

9. Which player tallied 8 assists in all competitions in 2012-13?

   a. Glenn Murray

   b. Yannick Bolasie

   c. André Moritz

   d. Aaron Wilbraham

10. Ian Wright left the Eagles to join which squad?

   a. Manchester United

   b. Manchester City FC

   c. Newcastle United

   d. Arsenal FC

11. Who appeared in all 38 games in the 2004-05 domestic league?

   a. Andy Johnson

   b. Joonas Kolkka

   c. Wayne Routledge

   d. Michael Hughes

12. Jason Puncheon played in all 38 games in the 2015-16 Premier League.

   a. True

   b. False

13. How many goals did Dougie Freedman score in the 2001-02 domestic league season?

   a. 20

   b. 16

c. 11

d. 8

14. Who won the club's Player of the Year award in 2019-20?

    a. Wilfried Zaha

    b. Jordan Ayew

    c. Andros Townsend

    d. Christian Benteke

15. How many appearances did Clinton Morrison make in all competitions?

    a. 391

    b. 377

    c. 343

    d. 316

16. Dwight Gayle earned 11 assists in the 2014-15 Premier League season.

    a. True

    b. False

17. Which season was Andy Johnson named to the Premier League PFA Team of the Year?

    a. 2002-03

    b. 2003-04

    c. 2004-05

    d. 2006-07

18. Who posted 6 goals in the 2014-15 domestic league?

    a. Marouane Chamakh

    b. Jerome Thomas

c. Jason Puncheon

d. Dwight Gayle

19. How many goals did James Vaughan contribute to all competitions in 2010-11?

a. 13

b. 11

c. 9

d. 7

20. Wilfried Zaha had made over 350 appearances for the Eagles as of May 11, 2021.

a. True

b. False

QUIZ ANSWERS

1. B – Wilfried Zaha

2. A – True

3. C – 8

4. D – James Scowcroft

5. C – Sheffield Wednesday

6. C – Dele Adebola

7. A – True

8. C – 368

9. B – Yannick Bolasie

10. D – Arsenal FC

11. C – Wayne Routledge

12. B – False

13. A – 20

14. B – Jordan Ayew

15. D – 316

16. B – False

17. C – 2004-05

18. C – Jason Puncheon

19. C – 9

20. A – True

DID YOU KNOW?

1. Crystal Palace forwards who have been voted the club's Player of the Year since the award was first given out in 1972 are: 1988-89, Ian Wright; 1989-90, Mark Bright; 2001-02, Dougie Freedman; 2003-04, Andrew Johnson; 2004-05, Andrew Johnson; 2015-16, Wilfried Zaha; 2016-17-Wilfried Zaha; 2017-18, Wilfried Zaha; and 2019-20, Jordan Ayew.

2. Scoring 21 times in 1905-06 in the club's first pro season to win the Southern League Second Division was Archie Needham, who played all positions for the side other than goalkeeper. Generally, an inside-right, Needham began his senior career with hometown side Sheffield United in 1901. He joined Palace in 1905 and remained for four years, playing over 100 games, and scoring 26 goals. He left in May 1909 to rejoin the Football League with Glossop but was back in the Southern League two years later when he signed with Brighton & Hove Albion. He then became one of the first pro soccer players in England to volunteer his services for World War I in 1915.

3. James "Jimmy" Bauchop of Scotland played just 47 games for Palace but managed to net 26 goals and led the quad in scoring in 1908-09 with 20 goals. He joined Palace early in 1908 from Norwich City after earlier playing with Glasgow Celtic. He became the first Palace player to get

sent off in a game when he was sent to the dressing room against Croydon Common in a London Cup clash in September 1908. Bauchop joined Derby County in May 1909 and continued to score consistently for several teams until retiring in 1924. His brother Willie Bauchop was also a pro soccer player before the First World War.

4. Inside-forward/center-forward John "Jimmy" Williams, who was nicknamed "Ginger," left Accrington Stanley in February 1909 to join Palace in the Southern League a few months later. He had no problem scoring goals, as he tallied 58 of them in 149 appearances in all competitions, including 5 in one game against Southend United in September 1909. Williams played with the side for nearly five seasons and was capped twice for Wales during this time. He joined Millwall Athletic in February 2014 and played until the First World War broke out, when he enlisted in the armed forces and served in France. Williams was reported missing in June 1916 and presumed killed in action, as reported by the *New York Times*.

5. Outside-right Albert "Bert" Harry played 440 games for the club and contributed 55 goals after joining the side in 1921. He scored twice in his debut in March 1922 and played 13 seasons for Palace. The side was relegated from the Second Division in 1924-25 and finished as 1928-29 and 1930-31 runners-up in the Third Division South to narrowly miss out on promotion. Harry played his final match for the club in March 1934 and held the team's appearance record until being surpassed by Terry Long in

1960, and later by Jim Cannon. He joined Southern League club Dartford in August 1934 and later tried his hand in France.

6. After graduating through the Palace youth ranks, Dave Swindlehurst kicked off his senior career in 1973 and went on to score 81 goals in 276 appearances for the club, leading the side in scoring twice and sharing the lead twice. He helped the team earn promotion from the Third Division in 1976-77 and then win the Second Division in 1978-79. He left for Derby County as a loan player in early 1980 and signed permanently with them in April. Derby paid £410,000 for Swindlehurst at the time to set a record fee for the club. He later played in Cyprus and returned to Selhurst Park in a coaching role until 2002.

7. Arriving at Selhurst Park from Millwall in 1992 just in time for the inaugural Premier League season was Chris Armstrong for a reported £1 million. He led the club in scoring for the next three eventful seasons as Palace was relegated, promoted, and relegated again. In January 1995, Newcastle United bid £4.7 million for Armstrong's services but it was rejected. Just two months later, Armstrong tested positive for cannabis and was banned for four games as the first Premier League player to fail a drug test. He was sold to Tottenham Hotspur for a reported £4.5 million fee in June 1995 after scoring 58 goals in 136 matches.

8. Journeyman striker Glenn Murray joined the Eagles in May 2011 after leaving main rivals Brighton & Hove

Albion. He netted just 7 goals in his first season but racked up 31 in 2012-13 to lead the team and place second to Watford's Matěj Vydra as Championship League Player of the Season. The club also won the playoffs that campaign to secure promotion to the Premier League. Murray played just 14 games in 2013-14 due to injury, only scoring once via a penalty. He was then loaned to Reading in September 2014 until Jan. 1, 2015. After scoring 8 goals in 18 league games for Reading, he returned to Palace and scored 7 goals in 20 outings. Murray totaled 47 goals in 126 appearances with the club before joining Bournemouth in September 2015 for a reported £4 million.

9. Andrew "Andy" Johnson was a 5-foot, 7-inch English international striker who joined the Eagles in 2002 from Birmingham City. He led the team in scoring for four straight seasons, from 2002-03 to 2005-06, and scored 32 goals in 2003-04 when Palace won the second-tier playoffs to reach the Premier League. Johnson was voted the team's Player of the Year for 2003-04 and 2004-05. He finished the latter campaign with 21 goals to lead all English-born players in the division, finished as runner-up in Premier League scoring, and was named to the PFA Premier League Team of the Year. Johnson joined Everton in 2006 but returned to Selhurst Park in 2014 and helped coach academy players. He left again in January 2015, after just one appearance and returned a year later to work as a club ambassador. Johnson was voted into Palace's Centenary XI in 2005.

10. Jordan Ayew, the 2019-20 Player of the Year for Palace with a team-leading 9 goals, originally arrived from Swansea City on transfer deadline day 2018 on loan for the season. He scored just twice in 25 games but signed permanently for a reported £2.5 million fee in July 2019. Ayew was also honored with the team's Goal of the Season Awards for 2019-20 and, as of May 2021, was still with the Eagles with 12 goals in 96 appearances under his belt. The Ghanaian international is the son of former Ghana captain Abedi Pele and brother of fellow Premier League player André Ayew.

CHAPTER 9:

NOTABLE TRANSFERS/SIGNINGS

QUIZ TIME!

1. Who was the Palace's most expensive transfer signing?

    a. Mamadou Sakho

    b. Christian Benteke

    c. Andros Townsend

    d. Eberechi Eze

2. Palace sold Chris Armstrong to Newcastle United for a transfer fee of £8 million in 1995-96.

    a. True

    b. False

3. Who was the Eagles' most expensive transfer signing in 2011-12, costing £603,000?

    a. Joel Ward

    b. Jermaine Easter

    c. Kagisho Dikgacoi

    d. Michael Chambers

4. Which player has the club received its highest transfer fee for?

    a. Alexander Sörloth
    b. Yannick Bolasie
    c. Aaron Wan-Bissaka
    d. Dwight Gayle

5. Crystal Palace signed Mamadou Sakho from which outfit?

    a. Paris Saint-Germain
    b. Southampton FC
    c. RC Strasbourg Alsace
    d. Liverpool FC

6. How much did Palace pay Queens Park Rangers to acquire Eberechi Eze?

    a. £16.02 million
    b. £18 million
    c. £24.6 million
    d. £27 million

7. The Eagles acquired six players doe £2 million or more each in transfer fees in 2013-14.

    a. True
    b. False

8. Who did Palace sell to Wigan Athletic for a fee of £2.70 million in 2009-10?

    a. José Fonte
    b. Ben Watson

c. Victor Moses

d. John Bostock

9. To which team did the Eagles sell Aaron Wan-Bissaka?

    a. Manchester United

    b. Liverpool FC

    c. Juventus

    d. Borussia Dortmund

10. How much did Palace sell Yannick Bolasie for?

    a. £22 million

    b. £26.01 million

    c. £30.24 million

    d. £34 million

11. Who was Palace's most expensive transfer acquisition in 2014-15?

    a. Jordan Mutch

    b. James MacArthur

    c. Wilfried Zaha

    d. Connor Wickham

12. Forward Dwight Gayle was acquired from Peterborough United.

    a. True

    b. False

13. How much was the transfer fee for Mamadou Sakho from Liverpool in 2017-18?

    a. £30 million

    b. £29.45 million

c. £27 million

d. £25.38 million

14. Palace sold Andy Johnson to which club?

   a. Everton FC

   b. AFC Bournemouth

   c. Fulham FC

   d. West Bromwich Albion

15. How much did the club sell Aaron Wan-Bissaka for?

   a. £37 million

   b. £42 million

   c. £49.5 million

   d. £52.25 million

16. Nigel Martyn was the first goalkeeper to be acquired for a fee of £1 million in English Football.

   a. True

   b. False

17. What was the transfer fee Palace received for selling Alexander Sörloth to RB Leipzig?

   a. £27 million

   b. £25 million

   c. £22 million

   d. £18 million

18. Palace signed Luka Milivojević from what club?

   a. Red Star Belgrade

   b. FK Rad

c. RSC Anderlecht

d. Olympiacos Piraeus

19. How much did the Eagles pay to acquire Christian Benteke?

    a. £33.5 million

    b. £32 million

    c. £28.08 million

    d. £26 million

20. Palace sold Jobi McAnuff to Watford FC for a fee of £3.5 million in 2007-08.

    a. True

    b. False

QUIZ ANSWERS

1. B – Christian Benteke

2. B – False

3. C – Kagisho Dikgacoi

4. C – Aaron Wan-Bissaka

5. D – Liverpool FC

6. A – £16.02 million

7. A – True

8. C – Victor Moses

9. A – Manchester United

10. B – £26.01 million

11. B – James MacArthur

12. B – False

13. D – £25.38 million

14. A – Everton FC

15. C – £49.5 million

16. A – True

17. D – £18 million

18. D – Olympiacos Piraeus

19. C – £28.08 million

20. B – False

DID YOU KNOW?

1. The top five transfer fees paid by Crystal Palace as of May 2021 are: forward Christian Benteke from Liverpool FC for £28.08 million in 2016-17; defender Mamadou Sakho from Liverpool FC for £25.38 million in 2017-18; midfielder Eberechi Eze from Queens Park Rangers for £16.02 million in 2020-21; winger Andros Townsend from Newcastle United for £14.04 million in 2016-17; and midfielder Luka Milivojević from Olympiacos for £13.59 million in 2016-17.

2. The top five transfer fees received by the Eagles as of May 2021 are: defender Aaron Wan-Bissaka to Manchester United for £49.5 million in 2019-20; winger Yannick Bolasie to Everton FC for £26.01 million in 2016-17; forward Alexander Sörloth to RB Leipzig for £18 million in 2020-21; forward Dwight Gayle to Newcastle United for £10.8 million in 2016-17; forward Wilfried Zaha to Manchester United for £10.58 million in 2012-13.

3. The biggest transfer fee Palace has paid for a player was £28.08 million to Liverpool for Belgian international forward Christian Benteke in August 2016. He finished his first season with the team as its top scorer with 15 league goals and 17 in total. Things went downhill quickly, though, as he netted just six goals over the next three seasons in 75 appearances. Despite this, Benteke signed a

contract extension keeping him at Selhurst Park until the end of the 2020-21 campaign. He bounced back in 2020-21 with 9 goals in his first 30 outings, giving him 32 markers in 145 career games with the club.

4. Palace sent their second-highest transfer fee to Liverpool when they purchased French international defender Mamadou Sakho for £25.38 million. He had arrived at the club on loan from Anfield in January 2017 to play out the remainder of the 2017-18 season. Sakho started well and was nominated for the Premier League Player of the Month award for March and was voted Palace's Player of the Month for the same spell. He signed permanently in August 2017 and was still with the side in May 2021. However, he had played just 75 times and scored only 1 goal.

5. Winger Andros Townshend started his career with Tottenham Hotspur after graduating through their youth ranks. However, he found himself on loan with nine different teams before being transferred to Newcastle United in January 2016 for £14.13 million. He then joined Palace in July 2016 for £14.04 million and signed a five-year contract after the club paid the release clause in his Newcastle contract. Townshend's goal in December 2018 against Manchester City was voted Premier League Goal of the Season for 2018-19. The English international was still with the team in May 2021 and had posted 16 goals in 183 outings.

6. In July 2013, forward Dwight Gayle was transferred to Selhurst Park from Peterborough United for £4.77 million and notched 8 goals in 25 appearances in his first season. He added 10 in 29 games in the next campaign and followed up with 7 in 20 outings in 2015-16 and helped the side reach the FA Cup final. Gayle won the Crystal Palace Goal of the Year honor for 2014. He led the squad in scoring in all three of his seasons with the club. He signed a contract in April 2016 to keep him at Palace until 2019 but was sold to Newcastle United just three months later, for a fee of £10.8 million after scoring 25 goals in 74 contests.

7. The biggest transfer fee Palace has received was the £49.5 million paid by Manchester United for defender Aaron Wan-Bissaka of England. He was a member of the club's academy since the age of 11 and began his playing days as a winger. Wan-Bissaka made his senior debut in February 2018 and was voted the team's Player of the Month for March and was named the club's Young Player of the Year for 2017-18. He continued his fine play in 2018-19 and was voted the team's Player of the Month four times and named the Player of the Year. Wan-Bissaka was then sold to Man United in June 2019 after 46 appearances.

8. Although he was born in France, forward Yannick Bolasie has spent his international career playing for the Democratic Republic of the Congo. Palace bought him from Bristol City in August 2012 for £567,000 and he helped the side win the 2012-13 Championship League

playoffs. He then netted 3 goals in a 4-1 away win over Sunderland to become the first Palace player to score a Premier League hat trick. He signed a 3½-year contract in 2015 and helped the squad reach the 2015-16 FA Cup final. But after 144 games and 13 goals with the club, Palace somehow managed to get £26.01 million for his services from Everton in August 2016. Bolasie played just 32 times with Everton before being loaned out for the last three seasons, as of 2020-21.

9. The Eagles also made another intriguing sale when they dealt Norwegian international forward Alexander Sörloth to RB Leipzig for £18 million in September 2020. They may have overpaid for him in January 2018 when they sent a fee of £8.10 million to Danish club FC Midtjylland, as he played just 20 times and scored once before being sent to Belgian side Gent on loan until the end of 2018-19. Sörloth was then loaned to Turkish side Trabzonspor in August 2019 until the end of the 2019-20 season and scored 33 goals in 49 games while leading the league and Turkish Cup scoring for the season. Sörloth's play in Turkey then enabled Palace to sell him to Leipzig for such a fine profit in September 2020.

10. Forward Wilfried Zaha graduated through the club's academy and made his senior debut in March 2010. He was sold to Manchester United in January 2013 for £10.58 million, making him the most expensive Palace player at the time. However, Zaha remained with Palace on loan until the end of the season and helped them win the

second-tier playoffs to return to the Premier League. He returned to Palace in August 2014 on a season-long loan and signed permanently in February 2015, helping the side reach the 2015-16 FA Cup final. The Ivory Coast international was still with the club as of May 2021, having scored 68 goals in 391 games, and he was voted the Football League Young Player of the Year for 2013, to the PFA Championship League Team of the Year for 2012-13, and Palace's Player of the Year for 2015-16, 2016-17, and 2017-18.

CHAPTER 10:

DOMESTIC COMPETITION

QUIZ TIME!

1. How many Football League divisional championships have the Eagles won?

    a. 7
    b. 5
    c. 3
    d. 1

2. Palace won the Southern League Division Two championship in its first professional season.

    a. True
    b. False

3. Which season did the team win the Surrey Senior Cup for the first time?

    a. 2002-03
    b. 1996-97
    c. 1990-91
    d. 1985-86

4. The Eagles played which club in their first FA Cup final?

    a. Liverpool FC
    b. Tottenham Hotspur
    c. Everton FC
    d. Manchester United

5. Crystal Palace reached the final of which competition in 1958-59?

    a. FA Community Shield
    b. London Challenge Cup
    c. Southern Professional Floodlit Cup
    d. FA Cup

6. Which round did the Eagles reach in the 2011-12 Football League Cup?

    a. First round
    b. Third round
    c. Fifth round
    d. Semifinal

7. The highest Palace finished in the top-tier First Division was 3rd place in 1990-91.

    a. True
    b. False

8. How many times did the side finish as runners-up in the London Challenge Cup?

    a. 10
    b. 6

c. 5

d. 2

9. What team did the squad face in its first Surrey Senior Cup final?

   a. Carshalton Athletic

   b. Wimbledon FC

   c. Sutton United

   d. Woking FC

10. What was the first season the Eagles reached the FA Cup final?

    a. 1956-57

    b. 1977-78

    c. 1989-90

    d. 1991-92

11. How many times has Palace reached the FA Cup final?

    a. 3

    b. 1

    c. 5

    d. 2

12. The Eagles won the 1940-41 London War Cup.

    a. True

    b. False

13. Which side did Palace defeat to win the 1991 Full Members Cup final?

    a. Nottingham Forest FC

    b. Middlesbrough FC

c. Southampton FC

d. Everton FC

14. How many times has Palace been a second-tier playoff winner?

    a. 9

    b. 6

    c. 4

    d. 1

15. Who scored the team's only goal in the 2015-16 FA Cup final?

    a. Yannick Bolasie

    b. Jason Puncheon

    c. Adrian Mariappa

    d. James McArthur

16. Palace has won two FA Youth Cups.

    a. True

    b. False

17. Who notched the winning goal in the 1991 Full Members Cup final?

    a. John Salako

    b. Alan Pardew

    c. Geoff Thomas

    d. Ian Wright

18. How many points did the Eagles post in 1905-06 to top the Southern League Second Division?

a. 26

b. 30

c. 37

d. 42

19. Which round did Palace reach in their first appearance in the Full Members Cup?

    a. First round

    b. Second round

    c. Fourth round

    d. Fifth round

20. The Eagles won the Fourth Division championship in 1960-61.

    a. True

    b. False

QUIZ ANSWERS

1. C – 3

2. A – True

3. B – 1996-97

4. D – Manchester United

5. C – Southern Professional Floodlit Cup

6. D – Semifinal

7. A – True

8. B – 6

9. A – Carshalton Athletic

10. C – 1989-90

11. D – 2

12. B – False

13. D – Everton FC

14. C – 4

15. B – Jason Puncheon

16. A – True

17. D – Ian Wright

18. D – 42

19. A – First Round

20. B – False

DID YOU KNOW?

1. Palace has had a long-standing, fierce rivalry with Brighton & Hove Albion that is known as the M23 Derby, which is named after the motorway which links the two locations. There are also rivalries with fellow South London clubs Charlton Athletic and Millwall as well as lesser rivalries with other London and area clubs, including Arsenal, Chelsea, Fulham, Tottenham Hotspur, West Ham United, Queens Park Rangers, and AFC Wimbledon.

2. The club has never won a top-flight English Football League divisional title. The side's best finish was third place in the 1990-91 First Division. The club has won two league titles in the second tier and one in the third. Palace has yet to win either an FA Cup or League Cup.

3. The team was crowned second-tier Second Division winners in 1978-79 and second-tier First Division champions in 1993-94. The side finished as Second Division runners-up in 1968-69 and won the second-tier playoffs to earn promotion in 1988-89, 1996-97, 2003-04, and 2012-13. The third-tier Third Division was won by the Eagles in 1920-21 and they earned promotion by finishing as runners-up in 1928-29, 1930-31, 1938-39, and 1963-64. The team has never won a fourth-tier league title but was promoted as runners-up in the Fourth Division in 1960-61.

4. As of 2020-21, Palace has been relegated from the Football League a total of eight times. The squad was first demoted in 1924-25 when it went from the second-tier Second Division to the Third Division South, which was merged into the Fourth Division in 1958-59. They were relegated from the top-tier First Division to the Second Division in 1972-73 and from the Second to Third Division the following season. The team fell again from the top-tier First to Second Division in 1980-81 and was relegated from the top-tier Premier League in 1992-93, 1994-95, 1997-98, and 2004-05.

5. The side has never won an FA Cup, but it reached the final in 1989-1990 and 2015-16. The Eagles also reached the semifinals in 1975-1976 and 1994-1995. The side won the FA Youth Cup in 1976-77 and 1977-78 and finished as runners-up in 1991-92 and 1996-97. Palace has never reached the final of a League Cup but made it to the semifinals in 1992-1993, 1994-1995, 2000-2001, and 2011-12. The club did win the Full Members Cup (Zenith Data Systems Cup) in 1990-91.

6. Palace's first venture to the FA Cup final resulted in a 3-3 draw with Manchester United on May 12, 1990, in front of 80,000 fans at Wembley Stadium in London. The game finished 2-2 after 90 minutes. Palace took the lead two minutes into extra time and Man United equalized with seven minutes remaining. A replay was held at Wembley five days later with another 80,000 fans in attendance. Lee

Martin scored in the 59th minute for a 1-0 Man United victory.

7. The 2015-16 FA Cup final was also contested by Crystal Palace and Manchester United and once again extra time was needed. The match was held at Wembley in front of 88,619 supporters who saw Palace take the lead through Jason Puncheon in the 78th minute. However, Juan Mata scored just three minutes later to send the contest to an extra 30 minutes. Jesse Lingard then notched the winner in the 110th minute to give Man United another cup triumph.

8. Crystal Palace had better luck in extra time at Wembley on April 7, 1991, when they faced Everton in the 1990-91 Full Members' Cup final in front of 52,460 fans. The Full Members' Cup was an English association football competition held from 1985 to 1992 and was also known as the Simod Cup from 1987 to 1989 and the Zenith Data Systems Cup from 1989 to 1992. The competition was created for the top two tiers of the Football League after the 1985 Heysel Stadium disaster, when English clubs were banned from European competition. Palace and Everton drew 1-1 after 90 minutes and Palace scoring three goals in extra time for a 4-1 victory.

9. Before joining the Football League, Palace won the Second Division in the Southern League in 1905-06 in its first season and finished as Southern League Division One runners-up in 1913-14. They were also crowned the

Football League's South Division Champions in 1939-40, Football League South Regional League champions in 1940-41, and Football League Division Three South winners in 1945-46. Those competitions were held during World War II when the Football League was suspended.

10. The Eagles have also won several regional titles over the years. They won the United League in 1906-07 and finished as runners-up in 1905-06 and they were also runners-up in the Southern Professional Floodlit Cup in 1958-59. The side hoisted the London Challenge Cup in 1912-13, 1913-14, and 1920-21 and finished as runners-up in 1919-20, 1921-22, 1922-23, 1931-32, 1937-38, and 1946-47. In addition, the Surrey Senior Cup was captured in 1996-97, 2000-01, and 2001-02.

CHAPTER 11:

CLUB RECORDS

QUIZ TIME!

1. What is the most points Palace has finished a season with?

   a. 94

   b. 90

   c. 85

   d. 72

2. The most consecutive games Palace has won in the domestic league is 11, from Feb. 9 to March 29, 1921.

   a. True

   b. False

3. The Eagles' biggest league victory was 9-0 against what club in 1959?

   a. Barrow AFC

   b. Crewe Alexandra FC

   c. Aldershot FC

   d. Walsall FC

4. Who is the oldest player to score a goal for the club, at the age of 39 years and 306 days?

   a. Michael Hughes
   b. Damien Delaney
   c. Kevin Phillips
   d. Gary Cahill

5. What is the most wins Palace has recorded in a season?

   a. 33
   b. 29
   c. 27
   d. 24

6. Who scored the club's fastest goal, in approximately 6 seconds?

   a. Cliff Jackson
   b. Simon Rodger
   c. Hubert Butler
   d. Keith Smith

7. The Eagles' record attendance for an FA Cup match is 32,832 in 1965.

   a. True
   b. False

8. Who scored the club's fastest hat trick, in 6 minutes and 48 seconds, against Wolverhampton Wanderers?

   a. Danny Butterfield
   b. Neil Danns

c. Alan Lee

d. Stern John

9. Palace's biggest league defeat was a 9-0 to what squad in 1989?

   a. Chelsea FC

   b. Oxford United

   c. Liverpool FC

   d. Barnsley FC

10. What is the most goals the club has scored in a domestic league season?

    a. 84

    b. 98

    c. 103

    d. 110

11. What is the fewest goals the Eagles have tallied in a league season?

    a. 18

    b. 24

    c. 31

    d. 45

12. The most games Palace has lost in a season is 31.

    a. True

    b. False

13. What is the most games the side has drawn in a league campaign?

a. 8

b. 11

c. 15

d. 19

14. Who is the youngest player to score a goal for the Eagles, at 17 years and 88 days old?

    a. Victor Moses

    b. Sean Scannell

    c. Wilfried Zaha

    d. Wayne Routledge

15. Palace's biggest victory in a League Cup game was 8-0 over what team?

    a. Torquay United

    b. Southend United

    c. Derby County FC

    d. Leeds United

16. Keith Smith scored the Eagles' fastest hat trick in a league match, in 8 minutes and 37 seconds against Hull City FC.

    a. True

    b. False

17. What is the fewest wins Palace has posted in a domestic league season?

    a. 10

    b. 8

    c. 6

    d. 2

18. The Eagles biggest defeat in an FA Cup match was 9-0 to which outfit in 1909?

    a. Queens Park Rangers

    b. Aston Villa

    c. Wimbledon FC

    d. Burnley FC

19. What is the most goals Palace has conceded in a domestic league season?

    a. 95

    b. 86

    c. 83

    d. 77

20. Wayne Hennessey of Wales has received the most international caps as a Palace player.

    a. True

    b. False

QUIZ ANSWERS

1. B – 90

2. B – False

3. A – Barrow AFC

4. C – Kevin Phillips

5. B – 29

6. D – Keith Smith

7. B – False

8. A – Danny Butterfield

9. C – Liverpool FC

10. D – 110

11. C – 31

12. B – False

13. D – 19

14. B – Sean Scannell

15. B – Southend United

16. A – True

17. C – 6

18. D – Burnley FC

19. B – 86

20. A – True

DID YOU KNOW?

1. The 15 players with the most all-time appearances for Crystal Palace are Jim Cannon, 660 (1973-1988); Terry Long, 480 (1955-1969); Albert Harry, 440 (1921-1934); Julián Speroni, 405 (2004-2019); John Jackson, 393 (1964-1974); Wilfried Zaha, 389 (2010-present day); Dougie Freedman, 368 (1995-2008); Nigel Martyn, 349 (1989-1996); Simon Rodger, 328 (1991-2002); David Payne, 326 (1964-1973); Paul Hinshelwood, 319 (1973-1983); Bobby Greener, 317 (1921-1932); Clinton Morrison, 316 (1997-2008); Bill Turner, 302 (1925-1936); and George Clarke, 299 (1925-1933).

2. Other appearance-related records for the club include most consecutive appearances, 254, John Jackson; youngest first-team player, John Bostock,15 years 287 days v Watford Oct. 29, 2007; oldest first-team player, Jack Little, 41 years 68 days v Gillingham April 3, 1926; and longest-serving manager, Edmund Goodman, 18 years, 1907-1925.

3. Team records for Palace include most league points, 64 (2 points for a win) in 1960-61 Fourth Division; 90 (3 points for a win) in 1993-94 Division One; most league goals, 110 in 1960-61 Fourth Division; biggest home league win, 9-0 v Barrow, Oct. 10, 1959; biggest away league win, 6-0 v Exeter, Jan. 26, 1935; 6-0 v Birmingham City, Sept. 5, 1987;

biggest home league defeat, 6-1 v Millwall, May 7, 1927; 6-1 v Nottingham Forest, Jan. 17, 1951; 6-1 v Liverpool, Aug. 20, 1994; and biggest away league defeat, 9-0 v Liverpool, Sept. 11, 1989.

4. Team seasonal scoring records include most league goals scored in a season, 110, Fourth Division in 1960-61; fewest league goals scored in a season, 31, Premier League in 2019-20; most league goals conceded in a season, 86, Third Division South in 1953-54; fewest league goals conceded in a season, 14, Southern League Second Division in 1905-06; 24, Football League Second Division in 1978-79.

5. Team records for consecutive achievements include most consecutive victories, 17, Oct. 14, 1905, to April 7, 1906; most consecutive league victories, 8, Feb. 9, 1921, to March 26, 1921; most consecutive league games without a loss, 18, Feb. 22, 1969, to Aug. 13, 1969; most consecutive league defeats, 8, April 18, 1925, to Sept. 19, 1925, and Jan 1, 1998, to March 14, 1998; most consecutive league games without a win, 20, March 3, 1962, to Sept. 8, 1962; consecutive league games scoring a goal, 24, April 27, 1929, to Dec. 28, 1929; consecutive league games without scoring, 9, Nov. 19, 1994, to Jan. 2, 1995.

6. Club highs for attendances at Selhurst Park are highest attendance for a top-flight game, 49,498 v Chelsea, Dec. 27, 1969; second-tier match, 51,482 v Burnley, May 11, 1979; third-tier contest: 33,160 v Queens Park Rangers, March 29, 1929; Fourth-tier encounter, 37,774 v Millwall, March 31, 1961.

7. Team lows for attendances at Selhurst Park are lowest attendance for a top-flight match, 9,820 v Birmingham City, April 11, 1981; second-tier game, 3,744 v Carlisle United, Feb. 1, 1986; third-tier contest, 2,165 v Newport County, Dec. 18, 1935; fourth-tier outing, 8,848 v Walsall, April 29, 1959.

8. The following are club records made in international competition while playing for Palace first capped player, Billy Davies for Wales, v Scotland on March 7, 1908; first capped player for England, Horace Colclough, v Wales on March 16, 1914; most capped player, Wayne Hennessey, 54 games for Wales; most capped player for England, 9, Kenny Sansom and Geoff Thomas; first player to compete in a World Cup tournament, Gregg Berhalter 2002, United States; first player to score in a World Cup tournament, Mile Jedinak, 2014, Australia.

9. Crystal Palace firsts include first match, 3-0 v New Brompton in a United Counties League game on Sept. 1, 1905; first FA Cup match, 7-0 v Clapham on Oct. 7, 1905; first Southern League match, 3-4 v Southampton Reserves on Sept. 2, 1905; first Football League match, 2-1 v Merthyr on Aug. 28, 1920; first match at Herne Hill Velodrome, 1-2 v Southampton on March 3, 1915; first match at The Nest, 4-1 v Millwall in August; first match at Selhurst Park 0-1 v Sheffield Wednesday on Aug. 30, 1924; first European match: 0-2 v Samsunspor on July 19, 1998, at Selhurst Park; first League Cup match 2-0 v Darlington on Oct. 12, 1960.

10. The highest and lowest overall league positions achieved by the club as of 2019-20 are highest Football League finish, 3rd place in the top-tier First Division in 1990-91; highest Southern League finish, 2nd place in the First Division in 1905-06; lowest Football League finish, 8th place in the Fourth Division in 1959-60; lowest Southern League finish, 1st place in the Second Division in 1905-06.

CHAPTER 12:

TOP SCORERS

QUIZ TIME!

1. Who has scored the most goals for Palace in all competitions?

   a. Ian Wright
   b. Mark Bright
   c. Edwin Smith
   d. Peter Simpson

2. The Eagles have never had a player win a top-tier Golden Boot.

   a. True
   b. False

3. Who led the side in scoring in their first Southern Division season?

   a. Stan Cubberley
   b. Dick Roberts
   c. Archie Needham
   d. George Woodger

4. How many goals did Christian Benteke score to lead the team in the 2016-17 Premier League?

   a. 7
   b. 10
   c. 15
   d. 17

5. Who led Palace with 15 goals in the inaugural Premier League campaign in 1992-93?

   a. Mark Bright
   b. Chris Armstrong
   c. Ricky Newman
   d. Grant Watts

6. How many goals did Clinton Morrison tally in the 2001-02 domestic league?

   a. 22
   b. 19
   c. 16
   d. 12

7. Ian Wright scored 24 of his 29 league goals with Palace while on his way to winning the 1991-92 Golden Boot with Arsenal FC.

   a. True
   b. False

8. How many goals did Edwin "Ted" Smith notch for the Eagles in all competitions?

a. 163

b. 150

c. 142

d. 124

9. Who led the side in scoring in the 2012-13 Championship League?

a. Wilfried Zaha

b. Glenn Murray

c. André Moritz

d. Jermaine Easter

10. How many hat tricks did Peter Simpson score in all competitions with the team?

a. 13

b. 18

c. 20

d. 26

11. Which player tallied 30 league goals in the 1960-61 season?

a. Cliff Holton

b. Andy Smillie

c. Johnny Byrne

d. Mike Deakin

12. Jordan Ayew led the Eagles with 9 domestic league goals in 2019-20.

a. True

b. False

13. How many goals did Ian Wright score in all competitions for Palace?

    a. 108

    b. 117

    c. 126

    d. 138

14. The most goals scored in a single domestic league match was 6 by Peter Simpson on October 4, 1930. against what club?

    a. Bristol Rovers FC

    b. Norwich City FC

    c. Brighton and Hove Albion

    d. Exeter City FC

15. What is the most league goals scored in a domestic season by one Palace player?

    a. 27

    b. 33

    c. 39

    d. 46

16. Six different players each scored 5 goals to lead Palace in scoring in the 2015-16 Premier League.

    a. True

    b. False

17. How many goals did Peter Simpson score in all competitions for the club?

a. 144

b. 152

c. 165

d. 179

18. Who led Palace with 27 goals in the 2003-04 domestic league season?

   a. Dougie Freedman

   b. Andy Johnson

   c. Darren Powell

   d. Danny Butterfield

19. Who scored 12 goals to lead Palace in the 2018-19 Premier League?

   a. Jeffrey Schlupp

   b. Max Meyer

   c. Andros Townsend

   d. Luka Milivojević

20. Mark Bright scored a club-record 56 goals in all competitions in 1987-88.

   a. True

   b. False

QUIZ ANSWERS

1. D – Peter Simpson
2. A – True
3. C – Archie Needham
4. C – 15
5. B – Chris Armstrong
6. A – 22
7. B – False
8. D – 124
9. B – Glenn Murray
10. C – 20
11. C – Johnny Byrne
12. A – True
13. B – 117
14. D – Exeter City FC
15. D – 46
16. B – False
17. C – 165
18. B – Andy Johnson
19. D – Luka Milivojević
20. B – False

DID YOU KNOW?

1. The club's top 15 scorers are Peter Simpson, 165 (1929-35); Edwin "Ted" Smith, 124 (1911-20); Ian Wright, 117 (1985-91); Mark Bright, 113 (1986-92); Clinton Morrison, 113 (1997-08); Dougie Freedman, 108 (1995-2008); George Clarke, 106 (1925-33); Johnny Byrne, 101 (1956-68); Albert Dawes, 92 (1933-39); Andy Johnson, 85 2002-15); Dave Swindlehurst, 81 (1973-80); Wilfried Zaha, 67 (2010, present day); Percy Cherrett, 65 (1925-27); Mike Deakin, 63 (1954-590; and Roy Summersby, 60 (1958-63).

2. Other individual club scoring records are: most league goals, 153, Peter Simpson, 1929-35; most goals scored in the FA Cup, 12, Peter Simpson; most goals scored in the League Cup, 11, Mark Bright; most goals in a season, 54, Peter Simpson, 1930-31; most league goals in a season, 46, Peter Simpson, 1930-31; most league goals in a top-flight season, 21 Andy Johnson, 2004-2005; most goals in a competitive match, 6, Peter Simpson v Exeter City, Oct. 4, 1930; most goals in an FA Cup match, 4, Peter Simpson v Newark Town, Dec. 13, 1930; most goals in a League Cup match, 3, Mark Bright v Southend United, Sept. 25, 1990; Ian Wright v Southend United, Sept. 25, 1990; Dwight Gayle v Walsall, Aug. 26, 2014; Dwight Gayle v Charlton Athletic, Sept. 23, 2015; Fastest goal, 6 seconds, Keith Smith v Derby County, Dec. 12, 1964; most hat tricks all

competitions, 19, Peter Simpson; oldest player to score a goal, Kevin Phillips 39 years and 306 days, v Watford, May 27, 2013.

3. Scottish center-forward Peter Simpson is the club's all-time leading scorer with 165 goals in 195 games and he also holds several other Palace scoring records including most league (153) and FA Cup goals (12) and most league goals in a season with 46 in 1930-31. He kicked off his career with Leith Amateurs in 1925 and joined the Eagles in 1929 from non-league Kettering Town. Simpson notched a hat trick in his league debut and went on to net a club-record 20 in his Palace career. He scored 37 times in his first season and tallied 54 in 48 matches in 1930-31, to help the team finish as runners-up in the Third Division South. Simpson led the squad in scoring in his first five seasons and played his last game for the club in April 1935 before joining West Ham United.

4. Second on the club's all-time scoring parade is Edwin "Ted" Smith, who scored 124 goals in 192 matches. The 5-foot, 9-inch English striker started his career with Brierley Hill Alliance in 1908 and made his way to Southern League Crystal Palace from Hull City in December 1911. Smith's pro career saw him play both before and after the First World War and he led the side and Southern League in scoring with 26 goals in the 1913-14 campaign. In fact, he led the team in scoring during the four seasons before World War I as well as in 1919-20 when competitive soccer in England resumed. He helped the team win the

Third Division title in 1920-21, which was its first in the Football League. Smith remained with the club until retiring in 1920.

5. England international Ian Wright left semi-pro outfit Greenwich Borough in 1985 to sign with the Eagles just before turning 22 years old. He scored 24 league goals and 33 overall in 1988-89 when the side earned promotion to the top flight by winning the second-tier playoffs. He scored twice 3-3 draw against Manchester United in the 1989-1990 FA Cup final, which had to be settled with a replay. Wright helped Palace finish in third place in the top flight in 1990-91 for their highest finish ever and scored twice to beat Everton to win the Full Members Cup the same season. He posted 117 goals in 277 games to rank as the team's third-highest scorer and in 2005 he was voted into the club's Centenary XI while being named its "Player of The Century." When he joined Arsenal in September 1991, the £2.5 million fee was an Arsenal record at the time. Wright is now a well-known TV pundit in the UK.

6. Mark Bright joined Palace for a reported £75,000 fee in November 1986 while Ian Wright and Andy Gray formed a striking partnership up front. However, manager Steve Coppell moved Gray to the midfield and formed a new striking duo with Bright and Wright. Bright was named to the PFA Second Division Team of the Year for 1987-88 and led the team in scoring with 25 goals. He helped the side win the Second Division playoffs in 1988-89 to reach the top flight and to reach the 1989-1990 FA Cup final while

being voted the team's Player of the Year for 1989-90. The club won the Full Members' Cup in 1990-91 and Bright led the side in scoring again the next season with 22 goals. He scored on the opening day of the 1992-93 season, which was the inaugural Premier League campaign but was sold to Sheffield Wednesday a few weeks later after contributing 113 goals in 286 games.

7. English-born, Republic of Ireland international forward Clinton Morrison kicked off his pro career with Palace after graduating through the youth ranks and scored a late winner in his senior debut in May 1998. He soon became a regular starter, notched 13 goals in his first full campaign, and led the side in scoring for four straight seasons with his goal total increasing each year to 24 in 2001-02. However, he was sold to Birmingham City in the summer of 2002. Morrison rejoined the Eagles in August 2005; he led the team in scoring again with 12 goals and followed up the next season with 16 goals to lead the side for the sixth time. He then joined Coventry City in July 2008 after netting 113 goals in 316 outings with Palace.

8. Striker Douglas "Dougie" Freedman of Scotland arrived from Barnet in September 1995 and notched 20 goals in his debut season to lead the team. This included an 11-minute hat trick against Grimsby Town in March 1996. He helped the side win the second-tier playoffs and reach the Premier League the next season. However, after just seven games in the top tier, he was transferred to Wolverhampton Wanderers. Freedman rejoined Palace in October 2000

from Nottingham Forest. With the club facing relegation in the final game of the season, Freedman scored a late winner over Stockport County to ensure survival. He helped the side win the playoffs in 2003-04 to return to the Premier League, only to be relegated after one season. He joined Leeds United on loan in 2007-08 and went to Southend United in 2008. Freedman scored 108 goals in 368 outings with Palace and returned in March 2010 as an assistant manager. He managed the side between 2011 and 2012.

9. Former miner George Clarke of England began his career with non-league Mansfield Town and then joined Aston Villa in 1922 for a reported £500 fee. The winger played just one league game with that club, though, and that didn't come until February 1925. Two months after that, he was signed by Palace manager Edmund Goodman. He then remained a fixture in the squad for the next seven seasons and led it in scoring in 1027-28 with 22 goals. Clarke chipped in with 106 goals in 299 appearances and set up his teammates for dozens more. He then joined Queens Park Rangers in 1933.

10. John "Johnny" Byrne scored 8 goals in 11 games for England and posted 101 goals in 259 matches with Palace to rank as the club's eighth leading scorer. Nicknamed "Budgie" due to his constant chattering, Byrne attended several trials at Selhurst Park while working as an apprentice toolmaker and was signed as a member of the ground staff. He debuted in 1956 as a 17-year-old and led

the side in scoring in 1959-60 and 1960-61 with 19 and 31 goals, respectively. His tally helped the side finish in second place in the Fourth Division in 1960-61 to earn promotion. He was sold to West Ham United in 1962 for what was then a Second Division British record fee of £65,000. Byrne rejoined Palace in February 1967 for a reported £45,000 and was sold to Fulham for £25,000 in March 1968. He later played in South Africa, where he passed away in 1999.

CONCLUSION

You've just enjoyed the chance to challenge yourself on the history of Crystal Palace from the team's 1905 beginnings up until 2021. What you have in front of you is the comprehensive story of the club in entertaining trivia form.

Because the club has been around for such a long time, it was impossible to include everybody and we apologize for that but hope that all, or at least most, of your favorites are included.

We hope you've enjoyed looking back at the team's colorful history in such a lighthearted and entertaining manner and we would be thrilled to know that you've learned something new while doing so.

Equipped with the content of a dozen chapters filled with quiz questions and "Did You Know" anecdotes, you should now be well primed to challenge fellow Palace and soccer fans to a plethora of quiz contests to determine who's the biggest know-it-all.

We've included as many of the team's top players and managers as possible and provided a wide-ranging collection of informative facts and trivia regarding the club's successes, failures, transfers, records, etc.

We also hope you'll be inclined to share the trivia book with others to help spread the word about one of England's most popular soccer teams.

The Eagles' flight has been a memorable one so far and there's still a long way to go, with several club goals waiting to be fulfilled.

Thanks kindly for being a loyal and passionate Crystal Palace supporter and taking the time to support the club by reliving its memories through our latest trivia book.

Printed in Great Britain
by Amazon

85669759R00079